I'm Not My Fault

I'm Not My Fault

Don Haury

AVON BOOKS ◆ NEW YORK

The Twelve Steps on pages 104-106 are reprinted and adapted with permission of
Alcoholics Anonymous World Services, Inc. Permission to reprint and adapt the Twelve
Steps does not mean that AA has reviewed or approved the content of this publication,
nor that AA agrees with the views expressed herein. AA is a program of recovery from
alcoholism. Use of the Twelve Steps in connection with programs and activities which
are patterned after AA but which address other problems does not apply otherwise.

I'M NOT MY FAULT is an original publication of Avon Books. This revised edition
has never before appeared in book form.

AVON BOOKS
A division of
The Hearst Corporation
1350 Avenue of the Americas
New York, New York 10019

Copyright © 1988, 1990 by Safe Place Publishing
Revised edition copyright © 1995 by Don Haury
Published by arrangement with the author
Library of Congress Catalog Card Number: 94-17185
ISBN: 0-380-77708-8

Library of Congress Cataloging in Publication Data:

Haury, Don.
  I'm not my fault / Don Haury.
      p. cm.
1. Self-esteem. 2. Self-defeating behavior. 3. Behavior modification. I. Title. II.
Title: I am not my fault.
BF697.5.S46H375 1995   94-17185
158'.1—dc20   CIP

First Avon Books Trade Printing: January 1995

AVON TRADEMARK REG. U.S. PAT. OFF. AND IN OTHER COUNTRIES, MARCA REGISTRADA, HECHO
EN U.S.A.

Printed in the U.S.A.

OPM   10   9   8   7   6   5   4   3   2   1

To my Brothers and Sisters . . .

This book is dedicated to "You,"
the most important and spectacular creation of all time.

CONTENTS

FOREWORD

Recently, I visited the maternity ward at a local hospital. As I stood with my nose next to the glass, looking at the rows of newborn babies, I was awed by their obvious vulnerability and innocence. How fragile and wholesome they seemed. I could not pick out one addict, robber, or street person; one murderer or wife beater; one manic-depressive, schizophrenic, or psychotic. Was I just kidding myself? Was I watching an illusion, under which lay the seeds of violence and disorder? I think not. Should you want to view the product of pure unconditional love, I suggest you come here, to see the purity of these tiny little beings nestled in their blankets. Hold them with loving care; feed and bathe them; keep them warm, safe, and secure; and the miracle of life will flourish before you.

But what happens and where do things go wrong? Could it be that some are secretly flawed, or are they changed by their environment and the behaviors of the people they depend on? Does the farmer blame the seed when his harvest is poor, or is he realistic enough to know that if he wants a healthy and productive crop, he'd better be attentive to soil conditions, weather, fertilizer, pruning, and the like, providing the care required?

I'm not naive enough to discount that there are genetic influences on everyone's character, but I do not believe that there are any "bad seeds." Although our society believes that some people are born bad, in each case the dilemma or disorder can be traced back to the soil conditions, weather, and fertilizer of a person's early life.

Most of my life, I felt like I was a "bad seed." I was led to believe that my growing environment had been ideal. A couple of years ago, I ran into other alleged bad seeds,

who had new perspectives. They suggested that my soil conditions might have been too rocky, the fertilizer too toxic,
the weather too cold. I could relate to how they felt and
what had happened to them. Ah-hah, I thought, maybe I
wasn't a bad seed after all. Just maybe, what I had been
led to believe was one big distorted lie, the result of a
devious game to protect the farmers. I set out on a journey
to determine the truth. My findings and conclusions follow.
Should you, too, feel as though you are a bad seed, I hope
you will read on.

Should you be a parent, I ask you to put that phase of
your life on the shelf for a moment and read the following
from your perspective as a child or young adult.

I'm Not My Fault

1

~

PROLOGUE:
THE SHAME-BASED CODEPENDENT
FALSE SELF

*"It's arrogant of me to think that
I am less than I really am."*

I am codependent. I believe the degree to which I matter
is proportional to how much I matter to others. I am de-
void of a healthy sense that I matter just because I am. I
depend on conditions outside of me to tell me who I am,
what I think, and how I feel; my identity springs from
what's happening in my life and the lives of those around
me. My codependency is the result of my having a false
self-identity, which means that I am missing a basic sense
of value, self-worth, and importance, the necessities for a
healthy, real self-identity. Consequently, I do not believe
that I deserve good things or success, or that I matter as
an entity unto myself.

TRAPPED BY SHAME

I am also shame-based. This means that I feel flawed and
defective, believing something is basically wrong with me.
Riddled with self-doubt, I constantly sense that I'm wrong
or that things are my fault. And, regardless of the circum-

stances, I don't believe that I have much to contribute or offer. Unreasonable fears are continual, especially those that relate to being judged or criticized. And, when push comes to shove, I don't sense that I have any rights. I try to camouflage who I am for fear that someone will expose me as an inadequate and defective fraud. I present myself as a capable, together person, in the hopes of deceiving those around me, and myself.

In relationships, I just can't imagine that a woman would like me just because of who I am. Nor can I imagine that someone would want to spend time with me, just because I'm me, without some kind of ulterior motive. Oh sure, if I had a big job or lots of money, or a big boat or expensive car, then I could understand. But no one will want me just because I'm an interesting and enjoyable person to be with. I counteract these feelings by behaviors that are supposed to indicate that I don't need anyone.

Some people might have a healthy positive identity, others might even have a somewhat neutral false identity that says "I really don't know about me." But not me. Mine is the identity of a shame-based false self, a "worth-less" self-perception that is almost entirely negative and subordinate to outside conditions. I struggle to believe that I have healthy attributes but I haven't even been able to generate a satisfactory relationship with myself. I criticize myself unmercifully, bound and determined to change my unacceptable self.

Everything and everybody seem to be more important than I am or than what I think and feel. I sense that I just don't matter much and that's okay with everybody else. Most everyone else looks better than I do, is more capable than I am, and more worthy. I try to tell myself this isn't true, that I am okay and capable and worthy, but a strong voice in my mind overrides me to say I'm not. And, if the voice doesn't persuade me initially, something I'll do or say will prompt it to say, "See, I told you so." Although I'm an adult, I often feel like a scared little kid in a big people's world. I feel that I am missing something it takes to make life work, as if I missed the class on Life 101 and there's no make-up course available. My codependent behavior stems from my subordinate false self-identity. My negative self-concept, my feelings of being "a-shamed" of who I am, come from the feelings my false self experiences when it has failed to live up to received expectations.

Shame can be defined as feeling that one's being has been judged by an authority as dishonorable or disgraceful. When I have what is called a "shame attack," I feel that my inadequacy, unimportance, and sense of being have been exposed for all to see. If someone sees this truth (as I perceive it), they see me as the nondeserving failure that I feel I am and I sink into a depressive sadness, my feelings spiraling downward until I cry out "What's the use?" Suicide then seems like a sensible solution. Most actions and decisions in my life have been an attempt to ward off or hide this false self from myself and everyone else. My shame and fears seem to feed off of each other. Together they eat away at me.

Somehow, I have felt that what I've done and who I have become is my fault. I didn't realize it was not true until I uncovered the cause of my shame-based codependency, which is rooted in how my false self was imposed on me, impeding the development of my real self.

What happens when I have this subservient or false self-identity? I amble about feeling badly about myself and who I am, and I face a continual struggle just to be okay, feeling sad, alone, and afraid most of the time. I believe I have caused my demise, feeling I have failed at living, ashamed of my failing. I really have contemplated suicide. After all, I don't matter much and no one would care, and nothing ever seems to work out for me. My life feels like an enduring series of problems to solve rather than an enjoyable mystery and a challenging experience.

I probably wouldn't be here today, except that the strongest natural instinct for human beings is survival. It seems that whether I like it or not, I have an inherent need to persevere. While my perceived truths about myself and my life were basically intolerable, somehow I needed to go on.

EASING THE PAIN

Fortunately for me, I found alcohol along the way. It was magic that eased the emotional pain, quieted the fears, and nullified my sense of shame. It allowed me to feel okay, alive, and seemingly normal for the first time. I didn't realize that my use of alcohol for emotional relief would lead me into a debilitating addiction. The pain of this solution eventually became too great, forcing me to give up the only solution I had found.

Since childhood I sensed, "If someone else could tell me I'm okay, then maybe I could believe it. Just maybe, if I could convince or prove to someone else that I'm important and worthwhile, then maybe I could convince myself also."

Acting on this reasoning, my codependency flourished. I abandoned myself in an effort to circumvent the feelings of inadequacy I had about who I was. And, since I had learned from the beginning that I had to abandon my real self to get my needs met and feel accepted, I didn't realize that I was giving up anything important. I had already learned and understood that *I* wasn't important and that I had to abandon *me* to get any positive validation or recognition.

Not able to find another option, I set out to make my codependent course work for me, living from the outside in, instead of from the inside out. In other words, I took everything learned from the demands on me that produced my reflective and responsive false self, and consciously began to hone my skills, reacting or responding to what was going on around me in my quest for recognition, approval, acceptance, and a sense of worthiness. Conversely, people with positive, healthy, and real self-identities, with self-worth and self-esteem, live life from the inside out, acting on or responding to situations outside themselves based on their inner beliefs and convictions, making intuitive, self-enhancing choices.

By abandoning me, I completely cut myself off from the

internal voice that intuitively knew what was best for me. Unknowingly, I was setting the course for a self-defeating voyage. I had begun the search for false gods.

Becoming hypervigilant, I was acutely aware of what others were doing or thinking as I attempted to manipulate my position, hoping to get positive validation and a sense of worth. I people-pleased, putting other people and things before me. I became vulnerable to anything that could make me feel better about me. I hoped beyond hope that someone would accept me, or tell me I was valuable, worthy, and important. Then maybe I could convince me. I didn't realize that no matter how much approval or acceptance I received from others, enough would never be enough until I was truly able to accept and understand the nuances of my perceived reality and family history.

I had entered the world of prostitution.

What others thought about me became paramount. I manipulated, controlled, lied, sacrificed, and compromised me, anything to improve my outside image and be recognized as a worthy, capable person. My image became who I was. I created fantasies and illusions about life and my relationship with myself and others. I became obsessed with anything that would help perpetuate my lie: alcohol, people, sex, work. I created illusion after illusion in an effort to produce a satisfactory self-image that would allow me to continue to escape my otherwise unbearable reality.

But all the while I knew, deep down inside, that I was a fraud and that nobody was home. Periodically, an unavoidable response to a life situation would confirm my truth to me. Some shame-based people I have known seem to be able to block out their negative self-perceptions altogether and continue to live as faultless images. They seem to have mastered the art of narcissistic self-righteousness, focusing completely on themselves and their position, blaming people and conditions for their feelings and anything that might go wrong in their lives. They never make mistakes or errors and don't have the capacity to say "I'm sorry." M. Scott Peck talks about them in his book *People of the Lie*.

At times I've tried that too, but my shame would eventually leach through.

Sooner or later, I had to fail in my desperate attempt to control and perpetuate an enlightened image of my disparaging false self. When I finally lost control, I reached despair. I could no longer deceive myself. I truly was a fraud and a failure, and there really was something wrong with me. The fear and hopelessness I felt at this point became the opportunity for a new beginning in my life. But I didn't realize it at the time.

HEALING THE PAST

My recovery from codependency and any other addictive or compulsive behavior is a function of healing my shame wounds inflicted in my family of origin, while nurturing and developing my real self.

I will make a statement that will aid your healing if you will allow yourself to believe it—"Who you are and what you've become is not your fault." I'll go on to say that you had no choice but to become who you are and to do what you've done—it couldn't have been any different. At birth, I believe you, like me, were dropped into a family that dictated who you think you are and all your subsequent behaviors and actions. Since then, you've more than likely been in somewhat of a robotic trance, replaying your family-of-origin experience. It gives credence to the statement "An unexamined life is not worth living."

I hope you can feel a little sadness or pain, or even get a little angry about that fact.

The following will show you how you might have become ashamed of who you are and inherited a self-defeating lifestyle. I hope it will help you to join me in saying "I'm not my fault."

2

UNDERSTANDING THE "WHY"

*"It would be egotistical of me to think
that I created my own demise."*

When I was born I was instinctively aware of the need for survival, the strongest drive in each of us. I sensed a need to be taken care of, a need for someone to feed and shelter me if I was going to make it. This need made me totally vulnerable to my original caretakers, Mom and Dad. Without them, I would die. The fear of abandonment is the primary, most intense fear of every child.

I assumed that my mom and dad were gods. After all, isn't a god a supreme being who is the creator and ruler of a universe? This sure defined my mom and dad—and my sister, who was three when I was born.

I had no idea that I was really a child of a Divine Creator who simply used my parents as vehicles to get me here. Their duty was to honor my preciousness, to nurture, love, teach, support and protect me. My bed should have been like a manger, and I was entitled to three wise men. I deserved gold, frankincense, and myrrh, too.

Instead, it was just "Give that kid a bottle every couple of hours and hope he doesn't cry all night and keep us awake. Cute though, isn't he, for a boy. Oh God, I didn't realize he'd be this much trouble, and that smell is just awful." "Come on now, coo and smile and make Mommy happy. When you cry and mess your pants you make Mommy sad, and sometimes mad."

Audacity is the word that comes to mind when I think about it. Mom and Dad not only implied that they were gods, they assured me it was true. My sister, acting as their designated disciple, concurred. Mom and Dad said I belonged to them, that I was *their* kid. They felt they had the right to tell me to do anything, to treat me any way they wanted, and to raise me to be whatever they wanted me to be. I believed them. After all, I had no second opinion or other logic on which to base another conclusion. So I became their property and they were my gods.

I lived by the gospel according to Mom and Dad. Their rules and regulations became my commandments. How they acted in my presence and how they treated me became synonymous with who and what I was. They used my older sister as a surrogate mother and watchdog. She had an additional agenda of her own that essentially said, "This kid's not going to steal any of my thunder, I'll make sure of that. He doesn't deserve it, 'cause I'm the important one." If Mom or Dad treated me as though I was bad, I knew I was a bad person. If they didn't pay attention to me, I wasn't worthy of attention. If they noticed only the things I did that they thought were wrong, I was inadequate and incapable. If they implied that I was in the way, I wasn't important. If they looked at me in disgust, I was disgusting. If they ignored me, I was nobody. The list goes on and on.

I didn't know they were playing with a stacked deck, that they were using perfection as the yardstick to judge my behavior. And they used blame as a tool to make me feel responsible for things that really had nothing to do with me.

ORIGINS OF THE FALSE SELF

I couldn't know they were promoting a false self in me rather than my real self. My false self inherently knows that it exists to satisfy the needs, wants, and issues of others. The validation, recognition, and acceptance I vitally needed came only when I was compliant and conforming to the needs, wants, or issues of others. I believed that their needs or wants were my purpose for existence.

The perceptions I formed about myself, derived from being judged by my mother, father, and sister, were the source for my beliefs about who I was. Rather than creating an environment where my real self could develop by nurturing, supporting, and encouraging expression of my special gifts and talents, my parents seemed interested only in my ability to satisfy their needs and issues. They molded me into what they wanted me to be.

My sister's interest, disguised under the role of a surrogate mother, was to make sure there was no room on the stage for me. In the name of my mom's and dad's professed expectations, she carried out her surrogate mother duties with malice. All three of them ignored or negatively judged my uniqueness and special talents rather than honoring and supporting them. No wonder I arrived into adulthood riddled with self-doubt; feeling lost, alone, and afraid; as a shame-filled, scapegoated rebel. Any attempt I made toward a true identity (or real self) was constantly denied, criticized, shamed, or ignored. The programming they instilled created a negative self-concept that was encoded on the core of my being. And no matter what I thought or did, it didn't change. I had ingested the poison of a fear and shame-based false self—the spirit of my real self was broken.

It's important to note how my parents' and sister's actions and messages reflected shame as opposed to guilt. Guilt arises from something we do, shame internalizes guilt into our very being, making it a statement and therefore judgment about who we are. Their behavior and responses toward me inflicted shame when I made mistakes, broke their rules, violated their beliefs, and failed to meet their expectations. My mom's, dad's, and sister's responses were judgments that told me there was something wrong with my very being rather than simply with what I did. Typical responses were:

"What did you do that for, stupid?"

"You're wrong."

"You're a bad boy."

"You should know better than that. What's the matter with you?"

These responses didn't let me know I was good, valuable, and okay, that I'd simply made a mistake and/or done something they thought was wrong in their opinion. They told me I was stupid, that something was wrong with me, and that I was bad.

UNDERSTANDING THE PAST

The following questions relate to how we were treated by our parents. I hope they will open a door to your awareness about the shame you might have and how your real self got suppressed in favor of a false or codependent self.

Answer yes or no. On a regular basis did your mom, dad, and/or a significant other . . .

	Yes	No
• support the fact that you were a precious, worthwhile person, even when you weren't doing anything?	___	___
• respect and support your ideas, beliefs, feelings, and space?	___	___
• spend time with you in an effort to teach and understand you?	___	___
• exhibit that they enjoyed being with you?	___	___
• take an interest in what you were interested in?	___	___
• go out of their way to help you, without your asking?	___	___

Yes   *No*

- understand that you were simply just being human when you made mistakes?   ____ ____

- stay with you while you were hurting, acknowledging that it's okay to hurt?   ____ ____

- confirm that you were okay, right where you were?   ____ ____

- accept you for just being you?   ____ ____

- spend time with you when you were frustrated, angry, sad, or depressed, and not tell you what you should do or how you should change?   ____ ____

- support you in doing whatever you need to do to take care of yourself first?   ____ ____

- support the fact that it's your life to live, encouraging you to explore the mysterious challenges of it your way?   ____ ____

The preceding questions relate to whether or not your parents were emotionally mature and secure enough to have the capacity to offer a meaningful love. "Yes" answers indicate the capacity to love, which produces a healthy sense of self and self-worth. If you have answered yes to most of the questions, you probably have a reasonably good self-concept—unless you are still in denial about what really happened in your family.

You might be protecting a "Fantasy bonding." Fantasy bonding is a survival mechanism we use when we need to create and believe happy illusions about our childhood. In order to go on living, we don't let ourselves see a disturbing truth about someone we desperately need. We instead make ourselves the culprits, making things our fault, taking on the guilt that doesn't belong to us. This bonding will persist as long as we "need" members of our family in any particular way. Fantasy bonding is part of the family trance, a state of mind that we develop when we're not emotionally capable of dealing with the truth about our history. It means we're still buying in to what our family wanted us to believe. If we're still in the family trance, we won't be able to clearly see the truth about our family-of-origin dynamics.

"No" answers symbolize neglect and emotional abandonment, indicating that you or what you think, feel, and do were considered of little or no value. These assumptions are the basis of your false self. The value of something or someone is indicated by its importance to another, the time one spends with it, and how one nurtures and takes care of it. "No" answers imply the formation of a false self, one that is contingent upon and subordinate to others' issues, needs, or desires, not one's own.

To see how your environment may have produced a more abusive and negative impact in your life, deepening the shame and enhancing the subordinate status of the false self, answer the following slightly altered questions.

On a regular basis, did your mom, dad, and/or a significant other . . .

	Yes	No
• support the fact that you were not worthy if you weren't doing something?	___	___
• discount your ideas, beliefs, feelings, and boundaries?	___	___
• exhibit that you were bothering them with your questions and your desire to understand?	___	___
• act like you were in the way?	___	___
• put down things you were interested in?	___	___
• chide you about your needing help, or offer to help only begrudingly and on their terms?	___	___
• leave you while you were hurting, saying that it'll be okay?	___	___

	Yes	No

- say or imply that you'll never make it being who you are? ____ ____
- tell you or suggest that you should be like someone else? ____ ____
- say to you when you were frustrated, angry, sad, or depressed that you shouldn't feel the way you do, then tell you how you should feel? ____ ____
- express the fact that it's not okay for you to do whatever it is you need to do to take care of yourself? ____ ____
- make it clear to you that your way of thinking was wrong and theirs was right? ____ ____
- make fun of and ridicule you? ____ ____
- defy you to get angry or to talk back to them? ____ ____

The preceding questions relate to whether or not your parents were toxic, meaning that their survival issues dictated their parenting efforts at your expense. Here, abandonment becomes betrayal, neglect becomes abuse, and shaming becomes soul murder.

Remembering that how you were treated determined how you feel about yourself, you might start seeing why you have negative ideas about who you are, and why you might feel worthless and unimportant, without rights. These messages set the stage for our feelings of fear and emptiness. They told us we were different, less valuable, alone, lost, and insignificant. They told us that no one is on our team, regardless of what we do. Answer the questions again for each significant person you have had in your life. Then you will better understand specifically who the culprits were or are.

ABUSE DISGUISED AS LOVE

The criticism from my mom, dad, and sister consistently put my very being under attack, instead of my behavior. They refused to give me healthy input. Although they professed to love me very much, their comments and behavior denied it altogether. I've since learned that words and intention don't matter, that it's behavior that signifies the presence of love. When abusive behavior is disguised as love, it sets up a confusing internal discord about what love is. We come to equate being loved with being abused, and we unknowingly set a painful standard for our future relationships.

If love has an opposite, it is shame, since love gives value and shame takes value away. Shame is about feeling like we've been judged a failure as a person, that we have failed at being what we were supposed to be. We become ashamed of who we are, what we know or don't know, and what we do. We sense that we are flawed and defective, that something is and has always been wrong with us. Unrealistic fears become our constant companions.

I can't tell you how many times I've heard the following:

> *"You shouldn't feel that way; what's the matter with you?"*
>
> *"Oh, come on, that wasn't a big deal."*
>
> *"I was only kidding. I didn't mean anything by it."*
>
> *"I don't know why you feel that way. I didn't say anything to hurt you."*

These statements fostered self-doubt rather than self-confidence. They told me that I shouldn't have felt the way I did and that my feelings didn't count or were wrong, challenging my reality instead of validating and supporting it.

As a child, I shut a door on my finger. I went to tell Mom that my finger was hurt. She looked at it, kissed it, and said, "Now it's okay, go out and play." I went out to play, but my finger still hurt. But my mom said that it was okay now. Since I was hearing this from one of my gods, it was truth. So I figured that something must be wrong with me, because it shouldn't hurt the way it did. I didn't know that feelings are not good or bad, that they just are and that they are a vital part of who I am.

Parents who feel the need to maintain control but don't possess mature, healthy coping skills often use "perfect" as the yardstick from which to criticize and judge their children. It's a suppressive tactic that allowed my parents to always seem right. On those terms, I could always be "had."

No matter what I did, it never seemed enough or right, as if they were bound and determined to keep me down, threatened by the possibility of my becoming a real person with rights, talents, value, and ambitions. They always made some sort of critical comment, even when I'd done something well. If I had done something well or truly performed admirably, and accolades came from outside the family, they'd say, "Oh, now you think you're hot stuff, don't you? You'd better not get too big for your britches." Or they'd imply that my accomplishment was a fluke.

My father's attitude toward me is expressed in two situations wherein he got me a summer job, at a time when I was near the top of my class scholastically, captain of the golf team, and a good, compliant kid, making every effort to do the right thing. In one job I reported to a guy who looked like an ex-sumo wrestler, loading hundred-pound sewer pipes onto trucks by hand. For the other job I scraped seeds out of pumpkins in the basement of a pie plant. Neither recognized or took advantage of the talents and intelligence I possessed, or the effort I was putting forth. Because his efforts both followed lengthy discussions we'd had about my future career endeavors, they conveyed to me what he, playing god, thought I deserved. My need to learn a little humility was one thing, his attempt to humiliate me was another.

Irrational expectations are another parental tactic, similar to the issue of perfection. Somehow, I was expected to know how to do everything, as in: "What do you mean you can't leap tall buildings with a single bound? Anybody can do that.'' I recall when my father, while coaching an older kids' baseball team, put me in to play right field in the last inning, when it didn't matter to the team. After the game and while driving home, he laughed at me and chided me about looking like I was chasing butterflies out there. It really hurt. Only a few years ago, when remembering the shameful feelings I had felt, did I realize that my father had never hit one fly ball to me and he had never taken the time or had the interest to show me one thing about playing baseball. We had never even played catch—yet he expected me to know how to play baseball. Once when we played golf, I hit a shot toward the green and my ball came up short, landing in a sand trap. He turned to me uttering his favorite expression—"What did you do that for, stupid?"—as if I'd done it intentionally. His comment implied that nobody would do something that stupid unless they had wanted to.

His unrealistic expectations still play a role in my life today. I have great difficulty believing that anything I do or accomplish is special or important or a big deal—if I can do it, anybody can. The fact that I can vividly remember these otherwise incidental issues, some thirty-five years later, indicates the impact they had on me.

I now see that my father protected his self-righteous stance by not risking anything. It's easy to play Monday morning quarterback when you've never played the game. He also professed what I call "blind loyalty," which he extolled as a virtue. I now see that it was used as an excuse to cover up his fear of risk or change. If one doesn't risk one can't fail or be criticized. I now know that failure is simply one's refusal or inability to risk or try again.

SOCIETY SUPPORTS DYSFUNCTION

Parents, limited in their ability to deal with a developing offspring, often want societal institutions to share their responsibilities. They feel the need for teachers, preachers, and the like to help discipline and mold their children, and blindly support whatever they dictate. No matter what, especially in my father's case, my teacher was right and whatever the preacher said was the gospel, leaving no room for human appraisal or questioning. Today, I know many people who are attempting to heal the emotional wounds they received from disciplines and doctrines blindly supported by their parents.

For many of us, it is difficult to identify how shame was caused in our families because most of the negative messages that judged us are commonplace in our society. A common family and social dysfunction is what I call the "Blame and Shame Game." It's become standard practice to blame others or conditions for what's happening or happened. Blaming the victim has become commonplace. The avoidance of accountability by responsible parties is the norm. And shame-based people, not knowing any better, get caught in the cross fire. I was often blamed for, and therefore made responsible for, situations and feelings that didn't belong to me, but I didn't understand that the game was unfair and twisted. I'm amazed at the power they accused me of having, when I had no rights, didn't count, and wasn't important. Phrases like the following scapegoated me, making me feel as though I was a bad influence or had a negative impact on others. I see their widespread use in our society.

> *"See what you made me do."*
>
> *"Now look what you've done; you hurt her feelings."*
>
> *"If it wasn't for raising you, I'd be successful today."*
>
> *"If it wasn't for you, I wouldn't be in the situation I'm in."*
>
> *"If I hadn't listened to you, it would have turned out okay."*
>
> *"Now look what you made me do. It's your fault."*
>
> *"I did it because of you. Now look what happened."*

The preceding comments, along with others like them, led me to believe I was responsible for what happened to others, a negative force, whenever I was present or involved. I could only conclude that life would be better if I stayed out of the way and that my very existence created problems for others. I've since had a continual tendency to fall prey to the blame game, picking up undue burdens, although today I'm much better at putting the monkey where the monkey belongs.

Looking back, I'm amazed at how "things" were even more important than I was. If I accidently broke something or had a household accident, my parents' initial concern was about what got broken or messed up instead of whether or not I was hurt or how I felt about what had happened. "Now look what you did" took precedence over "Are you okay?" I learned that possessions were more important than me.

Because I believed the many aforementioned circumstances to be the truth, the following unhealthy thoughts became a permanent part of my false self:

- I am always expected to know, or know better.

- I never feel welcomed or that I belong unless someone else says it's okay.

- I feel like a failure because I can't do what everyone else can do. I "s"hould "h"ave "a"lready "m"astered "e"verything.

- How dare I fail to be there for someone else, after all that person did for me?

- Who am I to think I have the right to ask you to support or help me?

- I shouldn't be afraid.

- I can't do (or say) that—it might hurt someone's feelings, and other people's feelings are more important than mine.

- How dare I think that I know what's right or what's good for us or me—I don't know what I'm talking about.

- It's not okay for me to enjoy myself.

- I should never put myself or my interests first.

- How dare I take care of myself—without considering you.

- I'm afraid I will look like a fool if I express my needs or wants.

- It's not okay to say "no," especially without a very good reason.

- I should be grateful for the little I get, because I really don't deserve much.

- It's not okay to play or enjoy myself unless I've taken care of everything I "should" do first.

- If I quit, I'm a failure.

Who we are is confirmed by how others treat us, and this validation becomes our self-concept, subject to further confirmation. Our self-concept then becomes the basis for our beliefs, from which we make our choices in life. A negative self-concept will foster unhealthy choices, setting a precedent for a self-defeating lifestyle. And since we live in a society full of self-centered fear- and shame-based people trying to hide their own shame and prove they're okay, our negative self-concept is frequently confirmed and supported. The more it is the more it becomes a seemingly indelible truth.

I cannot remember one instance wherein my mother, father, or sister admitted to making a mistake or being wrong about something. This behavior exemplifies shame-bound people, who try to hide or cover up shame at another's expense. Sarcasm and cynicism disguised as kidding were the norm; humor always denigrated someone else.

WE SEEK OUT WHAT WE ALREADY KNOW

When I went off to participate in society, church, school, and to be with friends, I hoped to discover that my opinions about myself were not true. I didn't realize that I would always gravitate toward the "familiar," which is a derivative of the word *family*. I was naturally drawn toward people who behaved and treated me like my family did, simply because what is familiar is comfortable. How was I to know that the familiar would always be more powerful than something that offered change? I didn't have a clue about how trapped I was by the allure of the familiar.

My family attracted other people who acted like they did. I attracted people who either felt like I did or acted like my family did. Talk about a no-win deal! It was easy and natural for me to find people who would confirm that I was bad, unimportant, and not good enough, which in turn confirmed my shame-based false self-identity. This verification, coming from outside of my family, assured me that the messages I had received from my mom, dad, and sister were correct. The validation made my fears true, and my fears increased. Many of us have experienced a particular incident or event with someone outside our family, yet "familiar"; something that confirmed that we should be ashamed of who we are.

I didn't realize that my parents and friends were living with the same kind of reality I was, which they were also desperately trying to hide. They didn't know what was going on either. And since they couldn't tell anyone about their shame and what they really feared about themselves, they put together a "this-is-who-I-am" act that became their alleged identity. They presented it to the world, hoping it would present an acceptable "image," continually adjusting it to suit the circumstances. By the time I came along, the "image reality" of their adorned false selves was all they knew. They were living in a world of illusions and images, with a "make-believe" identity, determined to make it real.

I was raised as an image, by two images. I had no other choice except to put an act together just like they had. No wonder I struggle today, trying to figure out who I really am.

The process goes on, generation after generation.

CONFRONTING THE FALSE SELF

During some recovery in a Twelve-Step* program, I found myself face-to-face with the shame issues of my false self. When confronted with the fourth and fifth steps, I was terrified. The fourth step says: "We made a searching and fearless moral inventory of ourselves." The fifth step: "We admitted to God, to ourselves, and to another human being, the exact nature of our wrongs." Oh no, I thought, now they want me to expose my inadequacy and worthlessness to myself, God, and others. Now they want me to expose the truth that I've been desperately trying to hide from myself and everyone else my entire life. My conclusion was: No way! My shame-ridden false self was the only reality I had at the time.

At a meeting where the topic was the fourth step, a person new to the program commented that she had curiously explored the fourth step. She said that she was afraid to tell anyone what she had determined, that when she looked inside to examine her inventory, she couldn't find anything or anybody. How frightening, to admit nobody's home inside, that we feel like a shell without substance.

As people ashamed of who we are, we create and protect a "make-believe" identity to counteract and hide our painful inner truth. We try to make dreams, fantasies, and illusions our reality and use any means to keep them alive.

If you, like me, learned in your childhood that little you think or do is acceptable or okay, you have probably looked around you in an attempt to find out what works for other people, hoping to mimic their behavior. I searched endlessly, hoping to find tools that would make my life work. I was always willing to compromise or abandon me for the sake of something or someone else that might change things.

I found myself with few convictions. I was generally willing to give up mine for your sake, or their sake, or whatever

*The Twelve Steps are property of Alcoholics Anonymous World Services, Inc.

sake, in an effort to be accepted or acknowledged, to belong or feel secure. No one supported or encouraged me to develop healthy boundaries or convictions for myself. They demanded that I abandon mine for theirs if I wanted to belong or feel loved. I relate all too well to the comment "If you don't stand for something, you'll fall for anything."

I was either blindly compliant or in unwarranted conflict with others, fighting for something without knowing what it was. I now know that my fight came out of my need for self-respect and the inherent quest for my real self, which I didn't know how to find. I've since learned that self-respect is an earned commodity, derived from standing up for one's own value system. It is a cornerstone of self-love.

I could not establish any healthy values because I was attempting to get my needs met in a family that expressed "conditional love," which really has nothing to do with love. I had to play the game, my needs intuitively told me that, but it was always by their rules, whether I liked it or not. Self-compromise and self-abandonment were inevitable.

In an effort to understand how you have compromised or abandoned yourself, complete the following phrases:

For the sake of . . .   *I had to, or had to be . . .*

- being or feeling accepted   _____
- feeling part of (belonging)   _____
- feeling cared about or loved   _____
- feeling secure   _____
- feeling free   _____
- feeling worthy   _____
- having fun   _____
- companionship   _____
- being liked   _____
- feeling approval   _____

For the sake of . . .   *I had to, or had to be . . .*

- material security   _____
- trusting or being trusted   _____
- emotional security   _____
- deserving pleasure   _____
- having intimacy   _____

My degree of self-esteem is inversely proportional to how much I compromise that which is in my own best interests. The more I compromise, the lower my self-esteem is. So, if I had to give up my human rights for the sake of getting my basic needs met, I could not gain self-respect or self-esteem. Your answers to the above questions will show you the areas where you compromised yourself, preventing a healthy sense of self, self-respect, or self-esteem.

Fill in the blanks again regarding your current situations, asking yourself, "For the sake of . . . I have to _____ (or) I have to be _____." This will help you to recognize areas where you continue to compromise (or sell out) yourself.

My shame-based codependent condition caused me to feel that I was inadequate and incapable. This "truth" seriously undermined my ability to survive on my own and compelled me to feel very insecure. My internal voice said, "If I am left alone with only my own devices, without help, I will not make it. I will not be able to take care of myself, by myself." The resultant feelings of fear were overwhelming, causing excessive self-centeredness. I needed to link up with someone who would help me survive. I became susceptible to anyone or any condition that I thought might help me to make it. In this vulnerable frame of mind, I ran a huge risk of falling prey to people who were only interested in using others. These people look strong on the outside, keeping their fears hidden while looking for a "hostage" to help them feel more secure.

If we have been able to develop a strong ego, called the

alter-ego, we become "arrogant know-it-alls" and victimizers. If not, we become "compliant subordinates" and frequently find ourselves in a victim role. Most of us bounce
back and forth between the two, feeling less than or better
than, but rarely equal to, those around us. It's interesting
to note that although these external personalities are oppo-
sites, the fear- and shame-ridden core of their false self-
identity is the same. The quest to develop the self-righteous
alter-ego is an attempt to avoid the depressive, shame-ridden reality of the false self.

Shame-based people often become prey to other shame-
based persons. Sadly enough, some will attack the vulnerability of another in a desperate, unmerciful attempt to
prove to themselves and others that they are better or okay.
This cycle of shame protection is a cause for widespread
discord in our society, keeping us stuck in the problem.

There is hope for change and recovery.

RECOGNIZE YOUR OWN WORTH

It began for me when I started to realize that I was a precious worthwhile human being, not because of what I did
or knew, but just because I was. We are human "beings,"
not human "doings," and we don't need to compromise
ourselves. We are entitled to be loved unconditionally and
are so loved by our Creator.

The negative judgment we've suffered is the cause of
our dysfunction, and it has made us doubt our human
preciousness. Love is judgment's opposite, validating wholeness and humanness. It confirms that we are special cre-
ations of our Creator, made in His/Her image and likeness.
Love tells us that we are deserving of joy, inner peace, and
oneness, just the way we are, as a given, not something
to achieve.

Love is not just a word. It is a state of being and an action
that honors, respects, and validates the preciousness and importance of oneself and others, without expectations.

If in reading this you've determined that you're involved

with people who do not respect who you are and your preciousness and Divine likeness, be aware that you are being used, abused, and judged incorrectly. You are being used to satisfy others' distorted needs, enabling them to shield their denial at your expense. This new awareness will be a step on a path to a better life.

I was taught that I was a subordinate being, that everyone and everything counted more than I did and therefore should be considered before me. A voice deep inside of me has screamed, "How dare I put me first and take care of me!" When I do, I feel like I'm doing the wrong thing, and very selfish. My goal has been to change this message and understand and believe that I have a right to my place on this planet, equal to anyone else. I am determined to stand for my rights of being, as accorded by my Creator, to honor my best interests and highest good. I am determined to embrace a new and profound truth that identifies me in Divine likeness, as pure love.

No person, place, or thing that is or ever has been on this planet is more important or valuable than you or I. Please join me on the journey toward believing this truth about both of us.

3

~

TOOLS OF RECOVERY

"The It I've been looking for is Me."

The long-term effects of the wounds from our past have left most of us without a healthy and enjoyable sense of self. We're riddled with self-doubt. If you, like me, don't feel any purpose or worth when you're simply taking care of yourself; if you believe that everyone will get mad, go away, or ask you to leave simply because you value your own needs; then we share the common burden of a shame-based codependent false self-identity. I hope the following suggestions will aid you on your journey to discover and celebrate the person you were meant to be, to find the enjoyable life you truly deserve.

EXAMINE YOUR CHILDHOOD

The journey out of our fear- and shame-based false selves into our real selves begins when we look at the reality of our childhoods. Your critical self-talk probably will tell you that your childhood wasn't that bad. It will tell you that Mom and Dad did the best they could, that you should forgive them and get on with it. This kind of self-talk honors the critical voices of our parents and older siblings, but ignores the expression of our inner children.

It is time to reverse the trend and honor the infant,

child, and adolescent voices in us, voices we have so long denied. These voices form the foundation of our real selves.

Feel free to experience and express your feelings of anger, pain, and sadness, as you unfold the truth about your family history. Write your feelings down. Talk about them with people empathetic to your cause. You might feel afraid or bad in doing so, but please continue with it. Expressing and acknowledging your feelings offers you a chance at finding your real self, maybe for the first time.

Know that to forgive without first experiencing and expressing your truth will trap you in your false self, negating your real self. After you have dealt with the feelings from your past, I believe you will gain a whole new understanding, one that will be your gateway to forgiveness.

I hope you can garner the necessary courage to confront the messages that denied your worth, your importance, your uniqueness. Doing so will give you the validation you have yearned for. It will allow you to own a new truth.

HONOR YOURSELF

Start focusing on yourself and what's good for you, instead of on others. Understand that you count and you matter. Acting on these principles may feel strange, but it's time to do whatever it takes to care for and honor yourself. I can't truly be there for anyone else unless I'm taking care of me first. I've said to myself, "Wouldn't anyone expect me to do whatever I need to do to take care of myself?" Healthy, caring people would. Those around you might not like it when you begin to take care of yourself. They will possibly get mad or threaten abandonment in response to your new behavior. Their responses essentially will be saying, "How dare you take care of you instead of me and what I want?" Know that you are a human being, not a human doing, that being you is enough.

ANALYZE YOUR SELF-TALK

Review the questions earlier in the book in an effort to see your role as a pawn in your family process. I trust this will permit you to begin recognizing your innocence.

If you question whether you've been mistreated or abused, examine the spontaneous voices in your mind. Do they criticize, judge, pick on you, and demean you, or are they supportive and on your team? If you're like me, they're critical and demeaning. We didn't dream up this negative self-talk. Our intensely self-critical attitudes could only have been learned from one source, the "gods" who raised us. You treat yourself exactly as you were treated. We mimic what was modeled to us. It's a natural response.

Take a "wait just a minute" inventory, searching your past for situations wherein someone or some circumstance told you that you were a worthwhile, capable person. We often forget these types of situations in the shadows of our shame-filled consciousness. I finally remembered two. At nineteen, I got myself a summer job doing drafting work at an engineering consulting firm. When I had been on the job for a month, the boss asked me if I would supervise an off-site project involving three other employees, overseeing a contract the company had received from the military. I was awed, then honored, by his request. The job went well, and when it was finished, he sincerely thanked me and commended me for the great job I had done. Similarly, but much later in life, a customer/friend of mine touted me as the best project engineer he'd ever seen. I tried to negate his comment, telling him I wasn't even an engineer, but he'd have nothing to do with it. He continued extolling my talents and capabilities, and the good I had done for him and his company. Ironically, I'd forgotten about both instances until I made an effort to remember them. I hope you can remember some too.

RECOGNIZE MISTAKES

Come to know that your "picker" is probably "broken." That is, you're not capable of picking people or situations that will respect you or value your best interests or your highest good. The people and situations you pick are more than likely "familiar" (meaning family-related). We choose friends and acquaintances who are similar to Mom, Dad, and our siblings, and pick work or social environments that mimic our family structure and the behavior within it. If you can identify the similarities between your past and present situations you will understand that you have been in a robotic trance since getting out of your family pinball machine. The day I realized I had many of my father's characteristics, I wanted to throw up. Then, I realized that I had married my mother, picked my father for a mentor, and chosen friends and business associates who mimicked my mother, father, and sister. I naturally gravitated toward work environments that repeated the behavior and attitudes of my family.

TRUST YOUR GUT

Now that you understand why your picker is probably broken, begin searching for your intuitive ability to make the right choices for yourself. Deep within you, underneath the familiar self-defeating voices, is an intuitive voice that will always tell you what is right and best for you. Your gut will let you know. Begin listening for this still quiet voice while instructing the others, "Shut up!" When dealing with another person, ask yourself, "Does this person have the desire or ability to respect who I am and honor my best interests?" If not, examine your involvement. Should the other party persist, feel free to say, "This just won't work for me," without explaining or feeling guilty. I've come to realize that "No" can be a complete sentence.

ACCEPT YOUR NEEDS
_____

Understand that what you think and feel counts. I rely on
the following to remind myself of my worth:

It's okay for me to . . .

- feel what I feel.
- want what I want.
- know what I know.
- think what I think.
- imagine what I imagine.
- see and hear what I see and hear.

   Although I'm entitled to the preceding, I cannot expect others to respond in kind. They have their own issues, equal to mine, which I need to honor along with
my own.

ASSERT YOUR RIGHTS
_____

Please know that you have the following human rights:

- To decide and discern for yourself what's best for you.
- To have your opinions and feelings respected.
- To feel like a capable adult.
- To feel and express anger. Anger is a healthy defense
  mechanism intended to protect you from danger.
- To change your mind.
- To make mistakes.
- To have worth and importance.
- To have fun.
- To be loved.

- To belong.
- To be free.

In accepting these rights, I've learned that I cannot make other people responsible for them, by demanding or expecting them to support me. However, those who have chosen to honor them, or be part of fulfilling them, have become my friends.

PUSH PAST YOUR FEARS

Overtly or covertly, our families taught many of us "Don't feel, don't tell, don't get close, and don't trust," in an atmosphere of control, secrecy, blame, fear, and shame. These dysfunctional messages led to our demise. Feel free to invert these lessons with supportive, safe people who will validate your new attitudes and perceptions.

A few years ago, while driving to a workshop on family-of-origin issues, I experienced a great deal of fear and guilt, not knowing what they were about. Finally, I realized they were in response to an old family dictate that said, "Don't you dare talk about us to others or expose our secrets. You'll pay for it if you do." I'm glad I pushed through the fears and continued on. It seems that every time I push through the how-dare-you fears of my family, I do something good for me.

ESTABLISH BOUNDARIES

My boundaries are invisible layers of energy or spirit substance that surround me at all times. In essence, they separate me from you, giving me a spot on the planet. They let me mingle with others while giving me control over how other people affect me. Boundaries protect me and my space, and I decide what to let through and what to keep out.

I can make my boundaries nonexistent, hard and impenetrable, or anything between. When I weaken them, I am more vulnerable; therefore I weaken them only to the degree that someone has earned my trust. I normally keep my boundaries mildly protective, letting me interact with others without being defensive. If someone accuses me or accosts me threateningly, I render my boundaries impenetrable, saying, "This is about them, not about me." I collect all information and comments directed at me in an imaginary bucket that hangs outside my boundaries. I use it as a place to inspect the material, determining what's healthy or unhealthy for me. If it's healthy, I bring it through my boundaries, into my being. What's left in the bucket is garbage, so I throw it away.

Unlike walls, boundaries let me interact on a feeling level while protecting me from those who haven't chosen to honor who I am. Walls protected me, but isolated me and promoted aloneness at the same time.

RECONSIDER YOUR VALUES

Understand that feelings of guilt are only applicable when you violate *your* value system. As codependents living in a false self, we often feel guilty when we fail to live up to another's expectations, or by their value system. The environment that instilled our subservient false self in us prohibited us from choosing our own values. Our parents insisted that their values become ours, which set us up to fail their declared expectations. Guilt then became shame and shame became who we are.

Examine your values and edit them to determine which ones make sense for you. Keep those you feel are pertinent to your beliefs and discard the rest. Learn to be attentive and true to those values you keep. Your ability to do so will be the basis for your gaining self-respect.

Move quietly away from people who have all the answers and those who freely give advice, blame, criticize, and judge. Those who exude self-righteousness and won't admit to making mistakes won't honor you or your best interests. They see you as an object, not the valuable human being you are. Although they may say otherwise, they will not accord you mutual consideration or respect.

I have continually been associated with people, or in situations, wherein my rights were not honored, yet my codependent behavior wouldn't let me break things off. A friend of mine says, "I seem to have hung in there long after 'good-bye' would have been appropriate." My response to my fears and shame have often clouded my ability to take care of myself. I now realize that when my fears and shame win, I lose.

DEMAND RESPECT

Disregard all comments that say "you should," "you better," "you ought to," and any other unsolicited advice. My silent credo is: "I demand that you honor who I am and recognize that I am a precious, worthwhile likeness of my Creator, no matter what I say, know, or do. I demand that you not criticize me, judge me, or give me advice, unless I ask. Then, only share your experience."

LOOK OUT FOR YOUR OWN NEEDS

Remember that we live in a fear- and shame-based codependent society, wherein dysfunction is the rule and the norm rather than the exception. Few people will honor you or your highest good. Most simply don't have the capacity or capability to do so. The majority of people are so preoccupied with counteracting their false selves that their need to prove, justify, or protect themselves leaves them little time for anything else. To counteract the widespread cynicism and sarcasm in our society, I've long had to guard against feeling wrong or bad by keeping my boundaries relatively strong. I can now see why I became so frustrated in my attempts to get from society the validation and support I didn't get from my family: everyone's on the defensive, convinced that the best defense is a strong offense. I've had to learn that I'm responsible for my needs, not others.

QUESTION AUTHORITY

Give yourself permission to question everything, both past and present. Feel free to reexamine the beliefs and rules of your family that were handed down as truths at the time. Most of the rules, beliefs, and ideals I learned from my family, religion, school, work, and social environments promoted suppression and control, or were a cover-up for these institutions' failings. I can't recall any lesson that supported enlightenment and freedom, honoring my uniqueness and gifts.

I define most religions as man's manipulation of spirituality in an effort to suppress and therefore control mankind. What better means to use than the "fear of God"? I've come to know that my Creator, or Spirit, or however one might perceive it, is pure unconditional love, without criticism, judgment, or any other negative input about me or what I do. I believe it is disappointed only when we fail to recognize and honor its "likeness" in ourselves and each other. And it doesn't care that I didn't capitalize the "i" in "it" in this and the previous sentence. That's not what love is about.

TAKE RESPONSIBILITY

Realize that although we were "victims" in our childhood, we have been "volunteers" in adulthood. When we see ourselves as volunteers, we realize we are responsible for our lives, choosing to play our parts. When we blame others for what we do or what's happening to us, we're being victims, stuck in the martyr role. When I blame, I surrender responsibility for my life, giving up my power over myself.

Then I'm demanding that someone else do something or change, so that I can feel better.

When I choose to be responsible, and acknowledge that I am volunteering to be a victim, I reclaim my power and can rechart my own course, controlling my own destiny. I view everyone other than children as volunteers. It helps me to reduce my unhealthy tendency to be overly "responsible for" and "obligated to" others. And it prevents me from falling into a martyr's trap.

When I see myself as a volunteer, I become accountable and responsible for the part I play. I can look at my motives and actions to see why I've involved myself the way I have. Only then can I realize what I need to do to effect change. It was hard for me to accept how much I, too, played the dysfunctional games of gripe, blame, criticize, and judge. When I saw how self-defeating they were, and learned a universal truth that says "We get what we give at the same time," I made a serious attempt to change my attitudes and behavior.

Two techniques helped. First, I removed the "to me" from any comment or behavior that I felt was directed at me. For example, if someone does something that prompts me to say "Why did you do that to me?" I'll change it to "Why did you do that?"—thus depersonalizing it. Then I can objectively look at why one might have said what they did without getting defensive. Doing so, in most cases, allows me to begin seeing that the particular issue is about them, not me.

The second technique relieves my spontaneous urge to criticize and judge. When I view someone doing or saying something I might have otherwise considered wrong, bad, or dumb, I say "Isn't it interesting what he [or she] needs to do to be okay in his [or her] own skin right now?" I then am amazed rather than critical, knowing that we're all just doing or saying what we feel we need to at any given time.

ADMIT THAT YOUR PAST IS IMPERFECT

Become aware of your relationship to self-honesty, and how often you might rationalize and justify your thoughts and actions, using them to mask self-deceit. Rigorous self-honesty is a cornerstone to healthy change, paving the way for self-esteem and self-respect. Most of my life, I've compromised what's best for me in favor of something I felt I needed or needed to do at the time. I didn't realize that when I compromise me or my truth, my self-esteem goes down the drain. It's true that "the truth will set us free." However, someone forgot to add that it also will probably hurt us or make us mad.

Admitting that I was very insecure and immature was very difficult for me, even though I was aware of my childhood history. As long as I was denouncing these truths, I was denying myself the opportunity to change them. My protective stance, guarding me from my shame, was keeping me stuck in a fantasy state, hiding from myself and others.

My journey toward an enjoyable real self has been a slow process of self-exposure, first to me, then to trusted others. It became much easier when I realized that I didn't create my demise. I began to look at my actions, not intentions. I learned to embrace the pain of revelation because I knew that knowledge would facilitate my growth. I began to question my motives regarding all of my actions. Did they honor my values? Was I being honest with myself? Was I honoring others? Doing so allowed me to begin to earn some self-respect. And once I gained self-respect, I could value the honest respect others offered to me, instead of debasing myself for a few moments of unhealthy approval.

ACCEPT A PROBLEM

At some point, your self-defeating thoughts, feelings, and behaviors may seem truly overwhelming. Or you may feel a "need to" or "need for" something that is causing you much grief and pain. Should this be the case, I suggest you acknowledge your dilemma by admitting that you are powerless over the situation or person. Doing so will offer relief, moving you toward solution. Surrender (or acceptance) is the step before a new beginning.

Not knowing better, we have sought outside help for an inside problem. With the help of the spirit living within us, we can claim the power we never had, take back the power we've given away, and chart a new destiny for ourselves.

SEEK OUT A HIGHER POWER

Explore your spiritual concepts of a power greater than yourself or of a supreme being and how you relate to it. Look back at how you acquired your beliefs and who taught them to you. Note how your concept of a higher power or God might be similar to your relationship with your parental gods. I have felt that I was supposed to be there for God, instead of God's being there for me, because that's how it was with my parents and sister. I have also felt abandoned and betrayed by God. Ironically, I feel the same way about my mom, dad, and sister. I've therefore had to discard the semantics that involve a god, because of my father's influence and the religion I was taught, which prevent me from experiencing the unconditional love I know exists. I now perceive the Spirit of Love to be an all-knowing, all-powerful spirit, there for me whether I'm there for it or not. I perceive it as an all-pervasive energy that supports me regardless of what I do or say, as a functional parent would have.

Believing in some kind of loving spirit that cares about me and will help me has been invaluable, especially since I've admitted to being powerless in several circumstances. However, if your history is anything like mine, I can understand your doubt about the existence of a supreme being that is truly on your team. Come up with your own version of what might work for you, and know it's okay. It's time you got the help and support you deserve. Feel free to demand it. Believe that it will work for you, not you for it, and see what happens. It may seem strange and scary, but I believe you'll be amazed.

I'm finally coming to understand what unconditional love really means. Unconditional love will be whatever we need it to be, supporting us as our needs, desires, and capabilities dictate, keeping our highest good as its primary objective. It will always be there for us, no matter what we say, know, or do. Having only experienced conditional love, I've had difficulty imagining and trusting those concepts, even though I finally know what they mean. There are universal principles and laws, but they arise out of love, not fear and shame (judgment). They are loving guidelines for healthy and harmonious living, such as: We get what we give at the same time; We can't cheat and win.

I feel fear writing the preceding, even though I believe its truth from the bottom of my heart. The voices from my past are screaming "How dare you!" "Who do you think you are!" "You've done it this time" and "Now you're going to get it!" They are promising pain and retribution for speaking against my authoritarian history. My courage to stand for my new beliefs, and for your sake, dictates my need to say it.

CONNECT WITH OTHERS

If you often feel a sense of "free-floating disconnect-edness," it is the result of your being separated from parts of yourself and the lack of healthy bonding. It started when your false self was nurtured into existence instead of your real self, forcing you to separate from the real you. A need for attachment to others is a futile attempt to solve the problem. We can connect to ourselves only by nurturing and supporting the real us, uncovering and dealing with the feelings and emotions that we've stuffed and ignored, while replacing our walls with healthy boundaries. As we connect more and more with ourselves on our journey toward wholeness, we will inherently sense a connectedness to our fellow human beings and to the Spirit of Love.

GROW SPIRITUALLY AND EMOTIONALLY

I believe that spiritual and emotional maturity are synonymous. Our relative state of maturity determines our relationships with others. The following represent healthy and mature attributes when dealing with others:

- Honoring differences with each other.
- Not taking sides.
- Giving equal consideration to both parties, with an equitable concept of "fair."
- Respecting another's position when stating one's own.
- Being able to withstand an emotional gut hit by responding instead of reacting or becoming immobilized.
- Acting in an honorable, accountable, and responsible manner.
- Valuing the "highest good" of all concerned as the primary priority.
- Delaying gratification.
- Understanding that there is no right or wrong, good or bad.
- Having one's rational mental state in control of one's emotions, needs, and wants.

I do my best to deal with others according to these ideas, and I use them to evaluate the way they deal with me.

Emotional maturity signifies that one's responses to life are determined by appropriate rational thought, not simply emotions. Immaturity suggests that one's emotions, based on one's needs, wants, or issues, direct behavior. Feelings just are. Emotions are feelings driven by a thought attached to them. Unharnessed or suppressed, they cause discord with others.

For example, I've been extremely defensive because of the authoritarian abuse in my life. I was constantly given advice and told what I'd better do. Not realizing that I was bringing up an old feeling and its corresponding thought, I've reacted defensively, attacking others who have offered me nothing more than simple suggestions. My responses were not appropriate considering only what was said. When I keep my emotions in check, controlled by a rational intellect, I recognize the difference between my history and my present, and I respond accordingly.

REDEFINE SUCCESS

Review your definition of "success" and where it came from. If it involves comparing yourself to others, you're going to be hurt and disappointed. Life is not about winning. One cannot win at life. Life is about living, a process that involves finding, exploring, and understanding yourself, evolving along your individual path. Its goal is enjoyment. My current definition of success involves a quest for inner contentment, peace of mind, and a lifestyle that promotes harmony, joy, and love. It doesn't have anything to do with what others do or become.

GET SUPPORT

Find some like-minded friends who are exploring the same issues you are. If it's feasible, find or start a "family of choice" support group or attend a healthy twelve-step meeting in your area. Twelve-step meetings include Co-Dependents Anonymous, Adult Children of Alcoholics, Alanon, and Alcoholics Anonymous, to name a few. Check local phone listings and newspapers, or ask around. Information regarding starting and running your own "family of choice" group is covered in Chapter 8. If you are recovering in a twelve-step program that doesn't or won't address the issues in this book, consider starting a meeting that does.

What I have talked about here is reality, what really happened in our lives. I realize that the persecutors were victims too, but that's no excuse. My intention is accountability and the exposure of ignorance, not blame. Having our reality discounted and distorted has hurt each of us. It's time for us to stand up for what happened, to recognize what we deserve and who we really are, honoring our feelings and respecting our own truth.

It is time for us to honor what has been discounted, realign what has been distorted, and recognize the beauty in ourselves.

You are as your Divine Creator made you in the very beginning. Your negative perceptions about yourself come from other's judgments, not from truth. Feel good about knowing that who you've been told you are is not the real you. Then begin your effort to free the beautiful person who has always lived inside you.

Should you struggle in the beginning, remember the others and me, who need you to walk with us, because we can't make this journey alone.

4

PUZZLE PIECES

*"Until we understand our own perspective,
we can't understand another's."*

This chapter is about situations I've encountered and
awarenesses I've had on my walk toward healing and self-
discovery. They've helped me piece together a new puzzle
about life, providing me with new perspectives that allow
me to see things differently than in the past. If you can
use a piece of my puzzle here or there, feel free.

Should some pieces not fit, that's okay too. Some of us
are more fear- and shame-based than others, and there
seems to be different manifestations in each of us, resulting
from our peculiar family environments. A real self might
be somewhat evident in some of us, still hidden in others.
I've noticed that a specific malady for me might not pertain
to another, although we share the same root feelings. Yet,
another's blind spots might be very clear to me. Deceit and
betrayal are main issues for me, abandonment for others.
Some of us had bonding with a parent, healthy or unhealthy, while I had little or none at all. The different
causes all had different effects, depending on how each
was perceived, internalized, and dealt with.

Should you disagree with my perspective, please know
you are not wrong, and neither am I. We are all entitled
to our particular viewpoint, absent of judgment. Someone
once told me that if we agreed on everything, there
wouldn't be a need for one of us.

CODEPENDENT VERSUS CONTRADEPENDENT

The word *codependent* has been used as a blanket term, like *neurosis,* to signify a general condition. It's been defined in various ways, often from a symptomatic perspective. In recognizing that the codependent self and an inferior false self were the same thing, I noted that my behavioral manifestations, and those of people like me, were different from others, even though we all agreed that we shared the basic shame-based codependent traits. Many people have a strong need to be attached to another in a relationship, based on a perceived hunger for love and attachment. I classify these types of people as classic codependents. People with this need are continually bouncing from one relationship into another, rarely without a partner. They have a high degree of vulnerability to others, and will rationalize any problems in favor of satisfying their attachment need. These people often pick victimizers, have a low tolerance for living or being alone, and are driven by their need to belong and be part of something. They continue to act out a fantasy love bonding they believe they had with a member of their family, one that made them feel safe and secure. I believe their primary issue is abandonment.

Although we have similar feelings and issues, I classify people like me as contradependents, under the umbrella term of codependency. We avoid close relationships because our history predicts that when we get closer to others we will incur pain. We perceive love as a painful experience, feeling more safe and secure when we're alone. I feel a natural resistance when I begin to get close to someone. This response is the direct opposite of the codependent's, who can't stand isolation. Those like me, who tend to promote isolation and detachment, have made a decision that "love is too painful, therefore I don't need it." Abandonment is not a strong issue with me; however, betrayal is.

A few years ago, I decided I would confront my father about his continual negative criticism and the put-downs he directed at me. The next time it happened, I confronted him, voicing my displeasure and demanding that he stop it, our future relationship depending upon it. At first he got angry, disclaiming his behavior, then he pouted, as I threatened termination of any communications with him. He finally said, "I thought we were closer than this." Wow, I thought, no wonder. Being close with my father means he's allowed to shoot me, and that's okay, I'll understand. Looking deeper into the dynamics of what being close or loving meant in my family, I could readily see why I opt for solitude versus attachment or belonging. To me, being close and belonging means that I have to give up my rights, compromise myself and what I want if I expect to get any of my needs met. My boundaries will not be respected. With a new perspective on relationships, and because my people-picker is changing, attracting healthier people, I am moving toward a healthier vulnerability in my relationships.

In summing up the differences, the classic codependents are extremely vulnerable to their need for intimate relationships, whereas the contradependents are extremely resistant to and afraid of them.

BALLS FROM THE PINBALL MACHINE

Some time ago, I came to realize that I have a variety of different voices in my mind, each having its own viewpoint about my daily affairs, who I am, and what I do. I discovered that I had one voice of an infant that just wants to be taken care of, but who felt neglected and hurt. Next came the voice of a young child who felt bad and in the way. Following that one, I had the voice of an older child, a good little boy, who said, "When we're good and do what we're told, no bad things or pain will happen." He'd do anything required to feel loved and a part of his family. Next came the rebellious teenager, who intuitively understood that what had happened to the younger kids was bad news, that they got screwed. His voice was resistant to advice and authority, determined to do it his way. He understood that no one was on his team and that he was betrayed

by people close to him. The remaining voices were repre-
sentatives of the voices of my mom, dad, and sister. These
critical and judgmental voices excited fear and confirmed
shame on an ongoing basis, making statements such as
"Watch out; you'd better not do that" and "I knew you'd
screw that up." They were never supportive or encouraging, always critical and demeaning.

The voices always seemed to be in what I call a "chicken
fight," arguing and bickering with each other. I didn't
know what to do about it, or which voices to believe. It
finally occurred to me that one voice was missing, that of
a mature, strong, loving adult in me to take charge of the
situation and deal with it in a healthy way. A mature adult
could nurture my infant; spend time with my young child,
letting it know that it's important; support the spontaneity
and individuality of my older child; support, understand,
and confirm the feelings of the rebellious teenager; and
send the critical parent and sister voices off to a rest home,
where they belong. Without a mature adult running the
show, I had the same condition in me that I had in my
original family—dysfunctional kids disguised as adults were
in charge. So I focused on creating the mature adult voice,
becoming accountable, responsible, self-disciplined, and
self-honest, whether I liked it or not. I confronted my rationalization and justification games, learning to parent my
inner children in a healthy, mature way. I do not believe
that we can do productive inner child enhancement work
without the presence of a reasonably healthy, mature voice,
running the show. Otherwise, we've simply got kids raising
kids again.

REDIRECTING THE ROLL

A relationship opened a new avenue of healing for me. A
woman friend and I, following a discussion about how neither of us was the other's type, entered into a male/female
relationship that lasted for nine months. We created the
potential for a healthy relationship when we agreed from

the beginning that our friendship was vitality important
to both of us. We agreed that no matter what happened
romantically we would each do whatever it took to honor
and protect our meaningful friendship. We were both capable of respecting this premise at the time, which is why
we're still good friends.

One day during a phone conversation, when she was
angry with me about something, she spontaneously said, "I
wish you'd stop being so damn nice and acting like my
dad. You're caretaking the little girl in me and she's not
involved here. Why don't you let the man out in you, and
say to hell with all this, I'm coming over to resolve this,
then taking you to dinner and bed?" Not having any of
the intentions she mentioned, I sat there listening in awe,
as she continued: "You must have been trained to be a
dad, not a male. That's why all the women we know think
you're so wonderful . . . You're so damn safe! A man would
be somewhat of a threat, doing his own thing irrespective
of others. . . ." I listened to the rest of her speech and then
said, "Do you have time to talk? If you do, I'll be over."
She did, I went over, and we spent the next three hours
unraveling a mystery in my life.

As it turns out, she was right. I was trained to be a dad,
not a male. Dads are caretakers; that's what my false self is
about. Development of my real self would have provided
for manhood, supporting my masculinity and male attributes. I made a decision: thereafter, I was going to be a
male, not a dad. At forty-eight, it was awkward to realize
that I didn't know how to be a male. Anytime I had made
an attempt within the constraints of my family, I had been
shot down and shamed.

Looking back at my teenage years, I deduced that if we
had been Jewish, my family would probably not have had
a bar mitzvah for me. Nobody honored or supported my
walk into manhood, or my sexuality. Suppressing someone's sexuality prevents their development as a male or
female. Sex was never discussed, although I somehow knew
it was bad. I recognized that my dad was more of a dad to
my mother than a husband. I can't recall witnessing any

male/female play between them. My mom and my sister were both my dad's little girls. Actually, my mom was his primary little girl, with my sister being her little girl. My mother was trying to live her life through my sister, giving her all the advantages she never had. Their triangle left no place for me, giving rise to my role as a lost child and scapegoat. I could only be in the way, to be blamed or to participate as a servant to their triangle. I was taught to caretake my mother's and sister's emotions while restraining my own. They were the queens of our hive. They in turn insisted that I take care of my dad's emotions, as well as their own. I was not recognized as having any needs and my dad didn't model maleness for me. Since he lacked the strengths offered by mature masculinity, he exerted his power over the only person available to him: me. I couldn't figure out why he never seemed to like me or get close to me. When I asked him what kind of relationship he had with his dad, he answered, "We didn't have one." Then I realized he treated me just like his dad treated him. To do it differently would have required him to experience the pain of his own childhood, which he chose to avoid rather than confront. Conditions of our history that we don't recognize and deal with get passed on to our offspring. Pain avoidance will perpetuate pain, generation after generation.

In looking back, I saw that my role in most of my relationships was fatherlike, wherein my needs didn't matter or weren't important. My false self-identity dictated my role, and I naturally attracted people who expected me to conform to their ideals. Today, I often see women who act as mothers, taking care of little boys in men's clothes, and men playing daddy to little girls in women's outfits. In both instances, those involved are mimicking what was modeled to them, acting out their respective roles, just like I did. I see few peer relationships between mature men and women. If you don't like what you're attracting, examine and change your role and your picker. Only then will you attract a different kind of mate.

My mother had the power in our family, having won the

codependent control war with my father some time ago. Thereafter, my father became a negative, passive-aggressive pouter, except when it came to me. My father's female side was strongly developed, his male side shut down. Conversely, my mother's male side was strongly developed, and she vacillated between exhibiting male characteristics and those of a little girl, lacking the development of a mature woman. In my natural quest for power and an identity, I adopted their traits. I've either attracted females with strong male tendencies, or helpless females with no male side at all.

I concluded that the feminine side of me was adequately developed, but the male side wasn't. I surmised that if I was to exist as a male, and encourage the development of my real male self, I needed to develop my male attributes. It was a key to moving out of my subservient false self-identity. Being aware that I was too fragile as a male, I focused on my need for emotional toughness and resiliency, expanding my male traits. In adopting the premise that there are no victims, only volunteers, I allowed my sexuality to develop, responsible only to my intentions and behavior. It was and still is an awkward process, because I struggle to feel any worth when I force others to own their part—resisting my caretaker role—and I am still learning that I am just responsible for taking care of me.

Irresponsibility is commonplace in our society, giving rise to most of the dysfunctional games we play. Few of us are willing or capable of owning our sexuality and expressing our feelings. Only when I saw myself as a voluntary participant in these dynamics and began to understand and deal with my issues of needing to prove, protect, and impress, did I move toward healthier interactions with others.

I've had a sense of guilt and shame about my sexual history. With nothing specific to indicate why, I just felt bad about everything. Finally, I decided to unwrap it in the hope of finding out why. In reviewing my sexual prowess, I couldn't find any reason that I should feel the way I did. I had never used any kind of force or even twisted a female's finger. So then why? I finally deduced that with my picker broken, I had fallen prey time and time again to women who refused to own their sexuality, who continued to give me a message that said, "I wouldn't have, if you hadn't wanted to," or "I only did this because . . ." I didn't wake up to the game until I became involved with a woman who said, "Of course, I like sex." What a revelation! It allowed me to look back to see how I had adopted guilt and shame, due to the irresponsibility of others. They were playing the role of victims, when in fact they were volunteers. I'm sure men play the same game.

WANTS VERSUS NEEDS

One evening, I listened to a woman who said she got her wants met instead of her needs, which caused great difficulty for her. Bingo, I thought, me too.

As a subservient false self, or shame-based codependent, my needs weren't acknowledged and I didn't matter much to those around me. Everyone else's needs counted, but not mine. I only got the responsibility for looking out for theirs. At times, my parents threw me delicious bones and table scraps, believing they were satisfying my needs. They appeased me rather than loved me, supplying wants disguised as needs. They were so involved with their own need to impress, prove, and protect, they didn't even recognize my needs.

I recall getting the biggest, most expensive Schwinn bicycle one Christmas, when I was thirteen. My dad felt very proud that he had bought it for me. I, too, was excited. I took it out for a test drive, all around the neighborhood, enjoying my newfound machine. Then, with my journey completed, I returned home, parking my bike in the driveway. I remember standing there, with that familiar empty feeling in my gut. The bicycle was supposed to make me happy, but it didn't, and I couldn't tell them. What's the matter with me? I thought. If I told them, they would have teamed up. "Your dad spent all that money on that bicycle, and it doesn't make you happy and appreciative. . . . What's the matter with you?" would have been the response, as it had been so many other times.

Bicycles are wants, not needs. The emptiness I felt in the driveway came from the absence of nurturing, care, understanding, compassion, healthy bonding, a sense of healthy connectedness, and the like, that were and are my basic needs. To replace them with things, such as bicycles, and imply that the things should accomplish the same results, is insane, incestuous abuse. I say "incestuous" because I see incest as the blatant and brutal violation of any personal boundary or right, not just sexual ones. In this case, as with many others, I was subject to mental and emotional incest.

I proved my supposition about wants versus needs a few years ago while visiting with my mom and dad. I had noticed they didn't have a radio/tape player in their condo, so I bought them one, giving it to them just prior to leaving for the airport. They didn't want to accept it. After they did, they insisted I take it back or allow them to give me the money for it. They continually talked about it all the way to the airport. I thought, Why are they making such a big deal about this? Then it hit me. By buying something for them, I was canceling out the things they had done for me during my visit, nullifying their expression of what they considered to be love. What a sad interpretation of love I thought. No wonder I feel the way I do and have my needs and wants confused.

I relate to the feelings of other incest victims, yet have no sexual violations in my history that I'm aware of at this time. I now know I am an incest victim, suffering from emotional, mental, and spiritual incest inflicted by the beliefs and behaviors of my parents and sister, violating my boundaries and rights. It was soul murder, leaving an indelible mark deep in my being, where the shame of my false self is rooted.

The programming I received says that I'm not supposed to have any needs, but I will get many of my wants met, and they are considered to be my needs. This internal travesty has caused me much pain and grief. For example, I expect to be able to spend money I shouldn't spend for things that I perceive might make me happy. But I'm not allowed to expect someone to have compassion to understand me, or to care about me, including myself. Sadly, even I haven't given my needs important consideration.

BROKEN PICKER DICKERING

In attracting people familiar to me, I have continually involved myself in unhealthy relationships in which our compatibility is based on my willingness to satisfy the other person's needs and wants. Healthy relationships are based on shared mutual interests and the enjoyment of being together. Two male/female relationships spurred my awareness of this condition.

In both cases, I sensed the woman's push for a deeper commitment from me, greater than the relationship called for at the time. I was puzzled by the pressure. I finally realized that their need for commitment had nothing to do with me, that I was a pawn in their game of "I need a committed relationship." Who it was with was secondary. Wow, I thought, no wonder my feelings about it weren't validated. I was blamed for my inability to make a commitment, when I could and would have if I had thought it was right for me. Following the respective break-ups, I predicted each would be in another committed relationship within thirty days. Both were, confirming my suspicions. Their being involved again, so soon after, was disrespectful of what we had shared, negating its value.

Similarly, I've had many so-called friends who appeared friendly and compatible with me as long as I was doing something for them, as long as I was filling a particular need or void in their lives. As soon as I stopped doing so, or their need or void was filled elsewhere, they'd go away.

I finally made a declaration that I would no longer participate in one-way relationships. If the relationship wasn't a two-way street, I wasn't going to play, no matter what. If people weren't going to be as supportive of my needs and desires as I was of theirs, I wasn't going to participate. No longer would I sacrifice my needs or desires for the sake of another's. Although I feared the loneliness I was predicting by my new stance, my commitment to my best interests enhanced the one friendship I had truly been missing, the one with myself. I then began to attract more compatible friendships. It seems that I have to make a commitment to me and close one door before another will open.

REAL OR THE ILLUSION OF REAL?

Having a shame-based codependent false self instead of a real self, I was essentially cut off from my intuitive connection to my soul and the essence of my beingness. Therefore, survival inherently became my primary issue, and I viewed it from the codependent perspective, looking outside myself for answers. Lacking an internal sense of self, I unknowingly gave my ego an exaggerated sense of power, since it was the only mechanism I had to draw on. My sense of my self therefore became my ego-consciousness.

Since the ego offers only a piece of the puzzle about life, giving it total control of one's life must create distortions and subsequent problems. The ego was designed simply to differentiate between the ethereal (spiritual) and material planes. Having come into this material plane as spirit, we needed a tool to distinguish between the two. Hence, the ego was designed in order to tell us that a traffic light is red or green, the stove hot or cold, and so forth. It operates like a computer, independent of the soul. We put experiential information into it, determine what it means, then get a corresponding reply. It tells us we are separate and different, and like a computer, it has only the ability to compare. It cannot recognize beingness, connectedness, oneness, a confluence with soul or spirit, and it cannot understand love. Therefore, by unknowingly giving the ego power beyond its domain, we are using only one limited source as the primary influence for our lives. And if the historical information imputed to the ego is distorted and abusive, the corresponding output will be equally distorted and tainted, setting the stage for self-defeating thoughts, feelings, and behavior.

With the ego-consciousness at the helm, lacking an intuitive real self, my well-being was always comparative. I bounced back and forth between "I'm better than" and "I'm less than," not having the ability to sense equality, connectedness, or oneness. Nothing ever seemed like enough, because the restricted comparative faculties of the ego are always using lack and scarcity as a yardstick. Bereft of a healthy sense of self or beingness, I felt the need to prove, impress, and protect. And since my false self was fear- and shame-based, I used my ego-consciousness to counteract the negative messages my false self gave me, to rationalize and justify that I was right, good, and okay, knowing deep down inside that I wasn't.

Some people seem to be able to block out the negative "deep down knowing" altogether. My personality alternated between egocentricity and depression. I became a master at comparing myself favorably, hoping my illusionary thoughts and beliefs were winning the struggle. However, when this facade got interrupted by what I've called "stark raving reality," where I couldn't void some shame-filled negative perceived truth about me, I'd sink into the depressive state of my false self-reality. It told me: "I'm nobody and I'm nothing," producing a shame attack. I spiraled downward to "What's the use," where I'd sit, hopelessly incompetent, and contemplate suicide. When this would happen, shame became an all-encompassing experience, and I felt wholly alone and afraid.

When we first gave the ego the power of decision in our lives, we began to make it God, even though it has no intuitive knowing or sense of connectedness. Our false selves gave it power because it sensed nothing else to draw on, since the intuitive, real self had not been given a chance to develop. We had to find some means to counter our shame-based false self-reality, or all the negative input we got would drive us to despair and death. Thus, we gave the ego power beyond its design, creating what some call the alter-ego, in which the ego is operating beyond its designated purpose, playing God. So began the illusions and lies.

I believe we become addictive if our real self is entirely denied and shamed, replaced by our depressive false self and our alter-ego. We search for something or someone who will make us feel alive, real, and connected. We create a fantasy reality in an effort to survive. We use it to counterbalance the degrading feelings our false self proclaims. I see my relationship with alcohol as an attempt to find my spirit and soul. I used it to quiet my fears and shame, and to perpetrate my make-believe reality.

The road to our real selves comes through the depressive side, not the ego side, because the despair, at least, is real. The depressive side results from our anger turned inward, the inherent feelings of futility that arise with the ego in charge, and the inherent frustration of being disconnected from our real selves. Our disconnectedness separates us from our soul and spirit, our fellow humans, and the all-prevailing essence of love.

The strength of my alter-ego is inversely proportional to the shame-based condition of my false self. It must be as strong as my self-worth and self-esteem are weak, offsetting them for the sake of my survival. If my counterbalancing ego-consciousness went away, my negative false self-reality would bombard me without recourse and I would consider suicide. Conversely, as I reduce my fears and shame, noting that my false self was a lie, while recognizing and developing my real self, my need for my protective alter-ego is reduced accordingly. My healing process is a continuing journey of whittling away at my fear- and shame-based false self, becoming real, while reducing the power of my alter-ego proportionately.

The ego has only discretionary capabilities, aimed at protecting us, giving us a sense of being separate and different.

Giving it power beyond its design sets up a conflict between our need for separation and our spiritual need for connectedness. The ego exists in the left side of our brain, the analytical part that concerns itself only with survival in the material plane. Using only this side in our lives is like trying to row a boat with only one oar. By itself, the ego will try to win at living—a futile exercise.

Our real self is comprised of two sides, the left side *and* the right side. The intuitive, or right side, recognizes connectedness and likeness, knowing that in a true sense we are all one, of one mind and spirit. It operates out of our soul. It understands that we are spiritual beings having a human experience, and knows that the ego is but a simple tool.

Letting go of the false self and its ego-based consciousness is the scariest, strangest, most awkward process I've encountered in life. How can we give up the only thing we know, when it includes our total identity? We naturally suspect we will be devoured by the fear and shame of the false self. That's why I believe it's imperative to understand that we did not create our demise, so that we can begin to relax our protective, defensive posture and deal with what happened to us, knowing it's not about us. The healing or recovery process is a progression of awkward bouts of frustration and anger (or depression) that lead to surrender (or acceptance), while building trust in an all-pervasive unconditional love, one that I am connected to, part of, and manifested from. The bouts of surrender are ego-deflation exercises, necessary to taking it out of its God-like role. I now recognize surrender as the step before a new beginning, wherein a new door opens to allow the dormant intuitive or real self to emerge.

It's been important for me to note that the ego-driven consciousness never did a satisfactory job in running my life. It predicted loneliness, created conflicts, and enhanced fear, all under the guise of protecting me. Recently, when faced with the loss of employment, I told a sage old friend of mine that my survival fears had kicked in, causing me some anxiety. He looked at me and said, "Haven't you figured out yet that survival's not a issue here?" How profound, I thought. I told him that I understood it on an intellectual level, but obviously not yet on an emotional level.

Balancing my uniqueness and difference with connectedness and oneness appears to be the means to a full understanding. I'm learning to be in the world, but not of it, choosing instead to embrace a new world I've discovered. It offers acceptance instead of achievement and judgment, love instead of shame, peace and harmony instead of conflict, abundance instead of scarcity, and joy instead of dejection. In one sense, you and I are uniquely different. In another, you are me, and I am you, and we are the water of the river of love.

DISCREPANCIES THAT CAUSE DIFFICULTIES (THE EGO AT WORK)

My natural aversion to pain is a basic part of my survival instincts. However, what happens if I expand this basic instinct to also avoid the emotional pain required to facilitate healthy growth? If my family environment produces continual and intolerable emotional pain, I will make just such an expansion. In adopting techniques that avoid pain altogether, I will lose touch with the reality of life, separated from it by my attempting to create a painless reality. In doing so, I will not grow emotionally. The total-avoidance dynamic is typical in dysfunctional families, wherein the parents dispense pain rather than the wisdom to cope with it.

Not knowing that a painful, shame-based false self was being inflicted on me by my parents and sister, I surrendered completely to my survival instincts, creating a pain-free, fantasy reality. In doing so, I became neurotic, a dweller in two realities. When my life in the fantasy world caused conflicts with the rules of my false self reality, I moved farther into fantasy. I defended my illusions at all cost, justifying and rationalizing as necessary. To expose them as a lie would have set off a chain reaction, exposing my entire belief system as a lie, confirming my false self messages that said I was a fraud. It would also have forced me to experience the pain that I was desperately trying to avoid. I did whatever it took to escape.

I have talked about two purported realities, the shame-based false self one, and the make-believe one. I suggest that two more exist. One involves a human being's real self, separate from the false self, which is simply perceived to be real; the other is a spiritual reality. As I continue to discard the negative false self issued by my family, and the fantasy reality I created to counteract it, I have come in touch with my real self for the first time. Since my real self has a soul, separate from the ego, I began to sense the existence of a complementary spiritual reality. The spiritual reality suggests that we are spiritual beings having a human experience. My journey has been a continuing walk into my real self, learning to experience the feelings I have so long denied, while exploring the reality of my spiritual essence. Balancing my real self with my spiritual self is my challenge, with life becoming more of an interesting mystery instead of the continual struggle to deal with fear, shame, and pain.

All conflicts seem to derive from disproportionate senses of what is fair. Anytime I'm dealing with someone mired in their pain-avoidance fantasy, conflict is inevitable.

I was in a conflict with my sister over my mother's estate following Mother's death. While her will requested equal distribution between my sister and myself, her money ended up in joint accounts with my sister. My sister was not willing to give me my equal share, offering instead a token settlement, as though it was all I deserved. A prudent but unequal settlement was finally reached just prior to my filing a lawsuit. I pondered why she acted the way she did, wondering why she'd treated me as though I was unworthy and undeserving of my mother's request. Although she claims she was a caring sister to me, my reality, supported by neighbors and a baby-sitter, says she was unmerciful in her behavior toward me.

It finally hit me. If one person treated another abusively and with disdain during childhood and didn't want to own up to what they had done today, wouldn't it make sense for that person to believe that the abused party didn't, and still doesn't, deserve anything better? Couldn't the abuser then continue to rationalize and justify his or her behavior based on a judgment that the other party wasn't and still isn't deserving or worthy?

I concluded that my sister's behavior was the result of just such a game, allowing her to continue to believe that I deserved her abusive treatment of me during our childhood. For my sister to see me as the wonderful and equal human being I am, she would have to own her actions and behavior toward me throughout our lifetime. Doing so would smash her justified, make-believe reality, forcing her to own and feel the guilt she tactfully avoids. Although she and her husband didn't need the money, she needed to support her fantasy reality.

To operate in harmony with our fellow man, with the ability to give equal consideration, we must break down our make-believe reality, separating our rationalizations and justifications from truth. Only then can we be open to what is equitable and fair. This becomes a major step on the journey to transform the false self into a real one. Owning our guilt, separating it from the shame, offers enlightening new perspectives when we realize that what we've done is not about who we are.

RELATIONSHIPS AND EMOTIONAL MATURITY

I mentioned earlier that I believe emotional and spiritual maturity to be synonymous. Our commitment to emotional growth shows our walk toward maturity, as a rational intellect begins to determine our behavior, instead of spontaneous needs, wants, and emotions doing so. Little kids cannot have healthy adult relationships simply because of their childish emotional condition. Being "childish" means having an immature, narcissistic emotional state, where one's emotions, driven by wants and needs, dictate one's thoughts and behavior, only from a self-centered perspective. Unfortunately, many people are looking for healthy relationships when their childish or immature emotional state prohibits that possibility.

I constructed a chart (see page 61), in an attempt to explain the dynamics of relationships to a friend so that he could see what is required for a healthy functional relationship. The chart relates the characteristics of emotional growth to functionality. I'd like to relate it to age, but can't, because of the prevalence of adults with childish emotions. The chart explains what we're capable of having, based on our emotional capability and functionality, using an arbitrary halfway line to differentiate between functional and dysfunctional. In reality, there is no line, but a gradual merge from one to the other.

The chart shows that if one's responses and behaviors are out of a fear- and shame-based, immature state, exhibiting blame, righteousness, competition, and the rest, one will be involved in relationships involving control wars, enmeshment, usury, acquaintances, and codependency. One's emotional state inherently predicts it.

Looking for intimacy, without a rational mature intellect in charge, can only foster usury, with both parties wanting and taking. It predicts that "I love you" means "I need you or need you to . . ." This scenario is the opposite of love, which exhibits giving without expectations. I use the following principles to define a healthy intimacy:

Intimacy—The capacity to share myself

- I maintain interdependency (not codependency), the recognition of my need for others without automatically expecting them to know what I need.

- I recognize and respect all three identities involved in the relationship: the other person, the relationship itself, and my own.

- I own my responsibility for my needs, wants, and desires without passing them on to others.

- I expect only mutual consideration.

- I have healthy boundaries and rational tolerance.

- I don't need to prove anything, impress anyone, or protect something.

- The degree to which I can be intimate depends on my ability to be vulnerable without being defensive; it is my capacity to risk who I am. That capacity is determined by:

  > my healthy sense of self
  > my self-confidence
  > my emotional maturity and capacity
  > my self-trust
  > my trust in the other person

Unlike intimacy, "enmeshment" suggests two people intertwined with each other, wherein their relationship clouds the individual identity of both. Enmeshed relationships cannot have intimacy, because there are no separate identities from which to share.

All three identities, (each person plus the relationship itself) need to be maintained and respected unto themselves for the relationship to have a chance at being enjoyable and healthy. One half person plus one half person does not produce two whole people. It produces enmeshment. My mother and father were enmeshed for over fifty years, their individuality clouded by it. They constantly argued and bickered with each other as their only way to sense separateness.

EMOTIONAL MATURITY/FUNCTIONALITY CHART

Emotionally Mature Adult
(Functional and Healthy)

[handwritten: ME]

CHARACTERISTICS
Trust-based real self
All-serving
Accountable
Humble
Complementing
Validating
Humanistic
Free
Honoring
Nurturing
Interdependency

ATTRIBUTES
Feels secure *[handwritten: sometimes]*
Acts considerately *[handwritten: always]*
Sees self as volunteer
Admits to mistakes and being human *[handwritten: yes]*
Values uniqueness/needs of others *[handwritten: yes]*
Supports growth through risks *[handwritten: yes]*
Allows for mistakes *[handwritten: yes]*
Gives others permission to be
   themselves *[handwritten: yes]*
Respects others *[handwritten: yes]*
Encourages and validates *[handwritten: yes]*
Responsible for self, respects the
   other *[handwritten: yes]*

RELATIONSHIP TRAITS
Loving   Friendly
Intimate   Interdependent
Trusting

- -

Narcissistic Childish Person
(Dysfunctional and Unhealthy)

CHARACTERISTICS
Fear- and shame-based
   false self
Self-serving
Blaming
Righteous
Competitive *[handwritten: VINCENT]*
Critical *[handwritten: Pete]*
Perfectionistic
Possessive
Shaming *[handwritten: VINCENT]*
Codependency

ATTRIBUTES
[handwritten: Pete] Feels threatened and insecure
Treats others as objects
Uses guilt to manipulate
[handwritten: Pete] Condemns and criticizes mistakes
Believes someone always has to lose
Builds self up by tearing others down
Judges mercilessly
Controls and suppresses mate with
   rage
Denigrates arrogantly
Needs others, fearing and hating that
   need

RELATIONSHIP TRAITS
Enmeshment   Superficial
Neediness   Control wars
Doubting   Codependent

I've adopted the following principles regarding my desire for healthy, mature relationships:

- Enjoy me, but don't need me.
- Can I enjoy, without needing, the other person?
- Do I enjoy, admire, and respect the other person?
- Does the other person enjoy, admire, and respect me?
- Do I have to compromise me to get my needs met?
- Do I have to compromise me to meet another's needs or wants?

I heard a man say, "My wife and I have a wonderful relationship. Should she decide to leave, for whatever reason, I will honor her choice. Although I will miss her, she will leave me with fond memories of the time we were able to spend together. And, I'll be able to enjoy those memories forever." How wonderfully healthy and mature.

The typical issue of dysfunction in relationships is the gripe-and-blame game, wherein neither party has the courage to do what is necessary to effect change. Expecting change without taking the steps that'll make it happen can't work. Blame and threats not backed up mean nothing. I've learned time and time again that no consequences equals no change. My resolve is exhibited only when I'm willing to take the actions necessary to support it. Otherwise, I'm whistling in the wind. Realizing the above and being willing to endure the consequences of my resolve have made the biggest difference for me. Although it's difficult, doing so earns my self-respect. When I'm griping and blaming, I'm wanting to have my cake and eat it too, playing the victim role, needing someone else to change for me to be happy. When I see myself as a volunteer, responsible for my part and willing to do what I need to do, it doesn't matter what another does. In doing so, I take back the power I have given away—and with it, take charge of my own destiny.

I've noticed that few people say what they mean or mean

what they say, and I'm included. We seem to have in-
grained dysfunctional communication in our society, so
much so it's become normal and okay. I've had fun playing
with our national greeting—"How are you doing?"—noting it as a classic example of a society that in general re-
fuses to shoot straight. It's spoken by almost everyone, and
is followed by the automatic response, "I'm fine." Asking
a question is not a greeting, and it exemplifies the many
distorted communication techniques we've adopted. I used
to get phone calls from friends who'd say, "I'm just calling
to see how you're doing," when in fact they were calling
because they were hurting and wanted to talk to me about
their problems.

In relationships, we tend to expect our mate to know
what we need or want without ever expressing ourselves.
We somehow seem to operate on the erroneous assumption "If you loved me, you'd know," as though anyone in
love inherently acquires psychic abilities. This assumption,
plus our inability to shoot straight, causes much confusion
and hassle. A friend of mine was saying that his girlfriend
phoned him to say, "I called to see if you felt like coming
over." How classic, I explained, of someone who's playing
a passive game of passing the buck, because she won't or
can't say, "I'd like you to come over tonight." Seeing how
I have fallen prey to this type of irresponsible, manipulative
communication, originating in my family, I began to force
people to shoot straight. Regarding the above comment,
I'd respond, "Oh, do you want me to come over tonight?"
diffusing the manipulative effort. If they'd vacillate over a
response, I'd quietly continue my questioning about what
they meant until they owned their stuff. If they refused, I'd
say, "Oh, well, I'll talk to you later," and quietly hang up.
I've learned that many people will get angry, refusing to
own their part, when quietly forced to. I could not enact
this philosophy until I stopped playing similar games and
learned to shoot straight with those around me. When I
realized that irresponsibility equals immaturity, I began to
own up to my behavior.

As a last note about relationships, if you've viewed the

chart with regard to what "they" need to do, you're in a narcissistic blaming posture, not willing to see yourself as a volunteer, accepting your part. If you see it as a guideline for your behavior and a simple discernment tool regarding what you might need to do, without blame, you're acting in a functional manner.

IS IT LOVE OR ISN'T IT?

I believe the word *love* is one of the most misused and misconstrued words in our language. The absence of love is so prevalent in most of us, we are inherently vulnerable to the desire to be loved. In being so, we are open to being manipulated. Many times I've heard someone say to another, "I love you," under the guise of "I need you," or "I'm using you, but if you think I love you, you won't realize it." Likewise, a comment like, "If you loved me, you would . . ." is generally inspired by our desire to have a narcissistic need satisfied by our mate, making another person inappropriately responsible for satisfying our needs.

We are either capable of love or we are not. There are no variations. It's either love or it isn't. Many behaviors, like "tough love," are simply self-justified behaviors used by people who don't have the emotional capacity to do the right thing. Love is the product of emotional strength and resiliency, not weakness. It is a choice and a gift to give.

Make your own determination the next time you hear "I love you," or you say it. In an attempt to provide us with another tool, I learned the following conditions of love, which show it as an action one might take, to have a productive value in another's life. Any one of the actions can produce any of the results i.e., "knowing" can produce "security," or "giving" can "reduce fear of loss."

Action	Result
Giving	Security
Being responsible (willingness to respond)	Pleasure
Respecting	Honesty and vulnerability
Knowing	Trust
Humility and intimacy (willingness not to assume)	Intimacy and caring
Courage (for commitment)	Reduced fear of loss
Caring	Understanding

Everywhere I look, the absence of love is at the root of every problem. In noting the problem, the solution becomes obvious.

If we have a distorted perspective about what love is, viewing it from an immature stance, we will not create the results we desire. My mother truly vowed that she loved me with all her heart, and I believe she did, from her perspective and capacity. However, her perspective of love was so clouded by her own issues and her lack of maturity, almost no love was conveyed to me.

SUBCONSCIOUS PERCEPTIONS EQUAL SUBCONSCIOUS BELIEFS

When I looked outside of my family to explore society, church, and school, I found them very similar to my family. All of my environments seemed to operate the same way, with similar philosophies, rules, regulations, and behaviors. If they were all the same, similar to my family, I unconsciously surmised that God must be like this too. In exploring the God concept at church, my suspicions were confirmed. There, too,

I was expected to be a subservient, good little boy. They taught me that I was a sinner* who needed to worship Jesus, God, and others while honoring Mom and Dad whether they were honorable or not. They told me I should be nice to my sister, and good. They implied that if I did it right and long enough, and looked and acted nice, I'd be forgiven and good things might happen for me. By this time, something in me resisted another philosophy that professed I was bad, requiring more servitude. Unlike my relationship with my family, here I had a choice.

I had established a subconscious belief system about God, and God's principles, based on what had been presented and taught to me and how the system responded to me. Therefore later on, in my search for answers about life, appealing to God was the last thing I considered. Along my road in recovery, when I claimed my right to question everything, past and present, I saw the difference between religion and spirituality. I saw the hypocrisy of religion and its use of spirituality for control of mankind. I determined that what I had been taught and therefore perceived as synonymous with a higher power, or God, had nothing to do with love. Yet I had heard that God is love. Something didn't add up. I concluded that what had been presented to me was nothing more than the collective ego-consciousness of those involved at the time. I had been taught a distorted perception about love simply to serve their purposes.

Today, thanks to my right to question everything, I understand a different, more plausible truth. I'm continuing to explore a whole new world, separate from the ego-consciousness, void of its sick beliefs and philosophies. My new world involves the presence of unconditional love, an all-pervasive energy that is everywhere and everything. With no history of unconditional love, I've had difficulty internalizing it as that place where harmony, peace, perfection, abundance, and joy abound, available to us all.

---

*The word *sin* comes from an old archery term meaning "missing the mark."

YOU'VE GOT TO BE KIDDING

I heard someone once say, "The good news is that it's probably too good to be true." The comment suggests our tendency to be skeptics, unwilling to accept information that might truly glorify our lives, choosing instead to argue for our limitations, making them real. In reflecting on the way we've been conned, I understand why.

Arnold Patent, in his book *You Can Have it All*, presented concepts about which I was unaware. They've provided me with some new and exciting perspectives. I didn't realize that I believed in principles such as "scarcity," thinking there wasn't enough to go around. I therefore felt the need to "achieve," just as my family and our society taught me. I also believed I needed to become, rather than be.

In his book, Patent did a masterful job convincing this skeptic that peace, harmony, perfection, abundance, joy, and love are a given, existing everywhere right now. They are not something to be achieved, but rather only to be acknowledged, accepted, and enjoyed. What a concept, I thought; I didn't know that.

I asked myself, "If this is true, why am I not experiencing them in my life?" I had thought their absence was due to my inability to achieve them, suggesting one more time that I just don't have what it takes. The next question became obvious: "If they are everywhere, for all to enjoy, what was I thinking or believing that was preventing them from being part of my life?" The light went on, bright and clear. My shame-based self-perception and my beliefs associated with my undeserving false self were my roadblocks. They were hindering me from experiencing these wonderful realities in my life. I was still believing what I had been taught about me and life. Having already learned that what I believe in, focus on, and nurture becomes real, I could understand that by believing in something like scarcity, I was making it real. I began to look at other similar issues in an effort to see where else I might be claiming or arguing for limitations, making them real only because of what I believed or had been taught.

Accepting my newfound truths, I proceeded to look for and remove the blocks rather than trying to achieve more. Each time I removed an obstacle, I was opening a door that would allow for peace, harmony, perfection, love, abundance, and joy to come into my life. At the same time, I began focusing on being, instead of becoming.

Some time later, I was encouraged to ask myself an interesting question: "Have I taken a vow of poverty or prosperity?" I was appalled when my answer seemed obvious: "Poverty." Becoming aware of what I unknowingly believed, I could understand why I struggled financially. I began to change my belief to prosperity, confronting the shame-bound thoughts and feelings that stood in the way. I am now on the road to believing that I, too, can have it all, realizing that I am limited only by my emotional capacity, self-discipline, and the fears and shame that still reside within me. My credo has become "When fear and shame win, I lose."

OH, REALLY?

I've talked about the difficulty I've had using the word *god* and gaining a spiritual perspective that could work for me. I listened to a tape that provided an interesting new viewpoint. At some point the man speaking essentially said, "You people just don't get it, do you? You're waiting around for the Second Coming of Christ, not realizing that the Second Coming of Christ is available to each one of you, any time you choose to pursue it. The Second Coming signifies the potential of the Christ state in each one of you." Wow, I thought, that's heavy and interesting. He went on to say, "Jesus was a man's name, while Christ signified his state of consciousness. The Christ state of consciousness is the highest state of consciousness attainable by mankind, and it is oneness with God. So, quit looking outside yourselves, waiting for the Second Coming, and start your own journey toward the Christ state of consciousness in each of you. That's what the Second Coming is about." I was somewhat amazed and appalled by what I had heard, but the quiet knowing in my gut suggested that what I had just heard was true. It felt right and made sense. It still does, even though I've changed the semantics of the situation for me.

As a footnote to the preceding, I think it's interesting to note that even our basic religious philosophy concerning "the Second Coming" comes from a codependent perspective, in professing that our solution will come from outside of us, instead of inside of us.

CAUGHT IN THE SYSTEM

So often in life I've become frustrated with the status quo of my family, social, or work situation. I've perceived most problems to be my fault. When one would occur, I'd immediately make comments to myself like "What am I doing wrong," or "If only I'd ... then ...," lacking the ability to realize that the real problem might lie with the dynamics of my environment or the people with whom I was involved. Somehow, I'd always make it about me and forget that it always takes two, that I'm only part of the problem. My family conditioning taught me that I was always wrong and it was all my fault, so I naturally assumed the same stance everywhere.

Most of us continue to walk down the path of "familiar," carrying our family training and roles with us, never realizing there might just be another road or outlook. If we could ask a fish about living in water it would say something like, "I don't know; I really don't have any thoughts or feelings about it." A fish couldn't have any thoughts or feelings about it, because it doesn't have any living experience other than water from which to compare. I knew a person who said he couldn't relate to being depressed. Later, he came back to me to amend his comment, saying he couldn't relate to depression because he's known nothing but depression his entire life. Likewise, a woman with whom I was having a relationship said that our relationship

seemed strange and awkward to her because she determined that it was the first nonabusive one she'd ever had.
My point is that until we have something to compare with,
we cannot know where we are or aren't, whether our environment is healthy or not, especially if it relates to our
family dynamics. Until I know what healthy is, I can't know
what unhealthy is. The same applies to functional versus
dysfunctional, abusive versus caring, love versus need, and
the like.

DIFFUSING TOXIC PEOPLE

I couldn't figure out how to confront shaming (negatively
judging), toxic people who somehow felt the self-righteous
need to issue verbal put-downs at me. Having moved past
the "I'll show you" stage, I wanted to avoid conflict or an
argument, but needed to deal with them. Now, I was only
interested in quietly protecting my boundaries and preventing others from shaming me. I had noted that toxic
put-down artists are masters of defense, extolling "That's
not what I meant," "I didn't say that," or "I was just kidding." They seemed to thrive on defensive arguments,
turning them against me, and I had to grudgingly admit
they were better at it than I was. The following situation
opened up a whole new way of dealing with this kind of
behavior. I call it "the game of innocent questions." To
play it, one needs to be able to respond, not react defensively or attempt to get even.
  An older retired gentleman I didn't know, who lived in
the same apartment complex I did, continually made sarcastic comments to me when we passed on the sidewalk or
in the parking lot. His comments were always disparaging,
similar to those I'd heard from my father. They included
statements like "It must be nice to be home at two o'clock
in the afternoon, when everyone else is working," or "Oh,
you're not working again today?" I felt his consistent attacks, and realized that if I told him I worked out of my

apartment, he'd just find another way to caustically chide me, like my father had done for a lifetime.

Having put up with his periodic comments for a few months, and realizing that he was a passive-aggressive toxic individual, I was determined to deal with him. One day, after he had dealt me another one of his sarcastic morsels, I stopped and ask him, "Excuse me, sir, is there something about me you don't like?" "Well, no," he replied. I responded, "Then why do you always feel the need to make belittling comments to me every time we pass each other? Have I done something to you?" Again his reply was, "No." I then continued, "You treat me just like my father did, and his negativity has caused me much distress and pain in my life. If I haven't done anything to you, why do you continually put me down the way you do?" His face turned beet red, and he stammered, "I need to go now," and hurriedly walked away. I got him, I thought, without recourse. I had exposed his game instead of reacting to his comments, causing conflict. Thereinafter, anytime we'd pass each other, he'd say something like "Hope you're having a nice day." With his game exposed, he either avoided me or said some abstract pleasantry.

I had learned a new technique, one that I could use anytime I didn't feel the need to attack or respond defensively. I now had a tool to defuse potential discord, solving the problem without conflict, instead of escalating it. I now feel free to ask probing questions like "Why do you ask?" or "Why did you say what you did?" or "What do you mean by that?" or "Why are you doing this [or that]?" forcing others to shoot straight, getting to the core of what's really intended or going on. In most cases, it exposes a manipulative game with a hidden agenda. I've learned that most hidden agendas involve another's issues being acted out sideways from a self-righteous posture. I've learned from my own responses that when anyone feels attacked or challenged in any way, the first response is defensive, immediately upgrading the conflict instead of providing an avenue toward solution. By asking innocent

questions, instead of reacting defensively, I avoid conflict
and expose any covert shaming games.

MY DISASSOCIATED SELF IN ACTION

Some time ago, before I realized the difference between
the false self versus real self perspective, I noticed that I
seemed to have two distinct realities, one relating to what
I thought I felt, the other some truth I didn't seem to be
in touch with. When someone would ask me to give a talk,
I'd say yes, not feeling any fear about what I had just agreed
to. Then, when on the way or when I'd get there, I'd be
terrified about what I had agreed to do, wondering whatever had prompted me to go along. What I thought was
my reality when I agreed wasn't my reality at all. Noting
this discrepancy and the differing effects, I began to question and confront how shut down I might be, out of touch
with my true feelings.

One day, while driving home from work, I was pouting
to myself about not having had a romantic relationship for
some time. I wanted one, darn it, and I deserved to have
one. Then I thought that maybe this was one of those cases
where I was feeling and thinking differently than how I
really felt about it. I decided to call my bluff. I imagined
that a friend of mine had called to inform me that he had
found the perfect female for me and that she was anxious
to meet me. He said they'd join me after work at a Denny's
restaurant, not far from where I lived. I pretended that I
had agreed. Now, in an effort to see what was really going
on with me, I changed my route, pretending that I was
truly on my way to Denny's to meet them, making it real.
The closer I got to Denny's, the larger the knot became in
my stomach. When I pulled into the parking lot, the fear
and knot I experienced told me the truth about why I
wasn't involved in a romantic relationship. I was terrified
of one.

Since that time, I have confronted many "that's no big
deal" comments I have made to myself and others by act-

ing as if they are real and happening right now. I've learned that only then can I tune in to what's really going on in me.

My false self's counteractive ego-consciousness and my real self's feeling reality are not in harmony because what I want isn't what I need, and conversely, what I need isn't what I want. My wants are a derivative of my ego, my needs a request of my soul. I believe that when my wants become my needs and my needs my wants, I'll be in healthy balance.

5

SETTING THE STAGE

"We can't give what we don't have."

Where do these abusive dynamics begin and what keeps them going for generation after generation? I feel sure that my parents were well-intentioned and that they wanted the best for my sister and me. However, they didn't understand that their best intentions couldn't counteract their actual messages and actions, the implications of which they were seemingly unaware. In hopes of creating a better understanding of how good intentions can produce terrible results, I offer the following perspectives on how my family stage was set.

My parents' ability to convey love was a prerequisite for my healthy development and growth as a child. Their ability to convey love was predicated on their own emotional maturity, their ability to recognize and satisfy my needs, to honor my best interests and highest good, without interjecting their own issues: that is the responsibility they had accepted in having a child. But they simply weren't capable of conveying love. Intent and desire didn't matter. With the best intentions, but without the most basic capacity, my parents could not create an atmosphere that would ensure my healthy development and growth.

BORN TO SERVE?

When my parents had me, and consciously or subconsciously expected me to fill a void, satisfy a need, or rectify a situation in their lives, I could not help feeling that my purpose for existence on this planet was to satisfy them, especially my mother. I could not realize that my true purpose for existence was to evolve unto myself for my own expression. Instead, I adopted a subservient identity and suppressed my real self, in favor of satisfying my mother's needs and expectations. My mother showed what she felt was love and care for me, but she was completely unaware of the damaging dynamics she created.

My relationship with my mother set the stage for my future. My concept of self-worth depended on how my mother looked at me, held me, and cared for me. Her behavior told me if I was valuable or not, and why. If my mother had truly been able to show me love, I would have decided that I was valuable unto myself, allowing my real self to grow. But I learned quickly that I existed primarily to satisfy my mother, and my false self flourished. Under those circumstances my self-actualization couldn't take place.

My mother's neediness and sense of deprivation overshadowed her intentions. Since her own self-critical voices said "Nobody's ever loved me" or "Nobody's ever been there for me," she used my sister and me to prove otherwise. Her behavior constantly asked the questions, "You do love me, don't you?" and "You'll be there for me, won't you?" These types of messages subtly but persistently told me that my mom's agenda was more important than mine. They impeded my chance to learn that I was and am an autonomous, wonderful expression unto myself, my only purpose to evolve.

A mother's request, such as "Oh, come on now, smile for Mommy," tells a baby how important it is to satisfy its mother. Similarly, comments like "When you do that, you upset Mommy," further define the baby's importance in terms of a parent's approval. Such a child will begin to determine its worth and whether it is "good" or "bad" by how others feel about its behavior. Some time ago, I was talking with a pregnant woman who said, "I'm really looking forward to having this baby. I think it's just what I need." Her statement suggested that her child was facing experiences like mine.

SACRIFICING MYSELF

As a baby and child, my desperate need for love and survival forced me to sacrifice anything necessary to fulfill these needs. Desperate for approval and affection, I abandoned my own self-actualization to satisfy my mother's conscious or unconscious needs. My environment simply didn't permit healthy growth and spontaneous self-expression. I therefore inadvertently pursued the development of my false self, the subservient, compliant, disassociated one, instead of my true self, which lay dormant and unfulfilled.

My status as a possession, rather than a person, was underlined by the often-used expression, "He's *my* kid." Later, directives like "You'll do what you're told, when I tell you to" reinforced my subservient role. My parents' responsibilities to me were never mentioned.

Naturally, I learned that I was unlovable when just being myself; instead, I was loved only for what I was supposed to be, first in an effort to satisfy my mother, then my father and sister. I realized that the conditional love I received would be removed if their needs and expectations were not continually met. I subjected myself to self-criticism and self-degradation anytime I supposed I had failed at my implied mission. After all, failure meant I was unlovable.

I lived by the idea: "If I am not compliant or needed, I am not lovable or valuable." This belief set up my long, painful codependent journey of living from the outside in, versus the inside out, reflecting on my environment rather than my inner beliefs and value system. Self-expression, self-acceptance, and self-love all became contingent upon something or somebody else.

Some years ago, noting what I thought was a newfound truth in my diary, I wrote, "Man will always gravitate toward where he is needed or wanted." It was my truth at the time, however sad and codependent it might seem. I still have a problem feeling valuable when I'm just taking care of me or when I'm just being. The lessons I was taught, and the subsequent validation of same, run deep.

The sad truth, whether I like it or not, is that my parents' childhood traumas were passed on to me, and mine to my children, consciously and unconsciously, regardless of our intent. I have continued the generational transfer of dysfunction. But I also investigated, understood, and addressed my own robotic trance, acquired from bouncing around in my family-of-origin pinball machine. I've learned that it's never too late to change the course, for myself or my children. The impact of our new awareness and change can truly influence the lives of others in a healing way.

6

THE DRAMA GETS ACTED OUT

"A slave is defined as a person owned by another, or dominated by some influence."

Now that I've finally reached some sense of rational maturity, I can see that my parents were generally immature, insecure people burdened by many issues of their own childhoods. They were codependent and shame-based, intent on counteracting the influence of their demeaning false selves. With good intentions, they more than likely had me because of some need or desire either or both of them had. The assumption that I was "their kid" suggested ownership—as if I were their slave—and their behavior confirmed it, precluding the thought that they understood their responsibility to me, my need for self-actualization, and the development process involved.

Having only the training of their own childhoods to reflect on, they set out to parent me, carrying their baggage and issues with them. Reaching into their bag of coping skills and beliefs, they pulled out a map that set us on a course based on fantasy beliefs about the parenting process and experience, trusting it would be like what they had imagined. For them it was a comforting ideal. Finally they were authorities. In fact they were gods. Their lifelong feelings of weakness seemed to vanish in displays of newfound power; their inferior shame-based selves had a chance to demand respect; at last someone would be there for them and do it their way. And, as creators in a new world, they had the opportunity to mold someone into whatever they wanted, or what they had always wanted to be.

When they had my sister, their coping skills and relationship were taxed, but they were able to cope with the process although they were somewhat threatened by the responsibility. Then, when I came along, stark raving reality hit and their coping skills and relationship were pushed to the limit. The bubble of their illusion burst. My very existence and my developing needs became a threat to them and their relationship. Instinctive survival traits replaced rational logic, and the Polyanna perspectives and good intentions faded away.

They understood, since they had learned this lesson in their own families, that if children have no value or worth, they won't challenge parents, threatening them with their rights and demands for acknowledgment. So they used the same behavior on me that had been used on them. With their own emotional survival at stake, they were not conscious of the damaging consequences of their behavior. The following terms explain the basic behavioral expectations in my family, used to keep me in line.

PERFECTIONISM

Evaluating any human being based on the standard of perfectionism isn't fair. After all, to err is human. Judged and criticized against this norm, I always came up short. The words that ring out of my past say, "You should have known better than that; what's the matter with you?" They suggested that there was something wrong with *me*, not with what I *did*. Nothing was ever enough. If I'd get a 90 on a school quiz, the response was "How come you missed ten percent?" as opposed to "That's damn good, all things considered." I couldn't know that perfection is an inhumane yardstick. I interpreted anything less than perfection as a personal deficiency. Looking back, I'm amazed at what I was expected to "know" or "know how to do," in spite of the little time anyone took to teach me. I still have a tendency to feel that something's wrong with me, when I'm just being human.

CRITICISM

Threatened by my development and growth, my parents criticized me unmercifully as a means of controlling me, instilling self-doubt rather than self-confidence. Self-doubt impeded my gaining a healthy sense of rational logic, keeping me off balance. Against the yardstick of perfection, I was pronounced bad, wrong, unworthy, and other negatives, at the whim of my dad or mom—or my sister, when she was playing the role of my surrogate mom. Their judgments attacked my being along with my behavior, imputing shame to me on a continuing basis. At times, when no condition for criticism or judgment existed, they would compare me negatively to another child. Since I didn't understand the game, the verdict was always "guilty as charged." Comments like "I wish you would act like Mary's boy" told me I didn't measure up and wasn't appreciated for just being me.

BLAME

This immature and irresponsible tactic was used extensively to make me feel guilty, because my parents and sister refused to be accountable and responsible for their own stuff. Not knowing any better, I became the innocent victim and scapegoat of their blame games. My mom, dad, and sister made comments like "It's your fault that I didn't . . ." or "Look at what you made me do," making me responsible for things I had nothing to do with. I ingested the blame as shame, believing that my very presence had a negative influence on others. I couldn't have known that I was a victim of a sick, irresponsible game; it was the only game

I knew. Subjected to this type of dialogue, I learned to believe that I had power, but only in a destructive capacity.

Worse, I believed their blame tactics to be acceptable behavior, and I practiced them too. I now see that this immature technique kept any of us in my family from maturing and becoming responsible adults.

RIGHTEOUSNESS

My parents, as erstwhile gods, professed that they knew everything, especially what was best for me and everybody else. They didn't honor any input from me regarding my wants or desires. In retrospect, I see this self-righteous stance as the height of audaciousness. But how could I have known they were wrong and that I should have had a voice in matters that concerned my life? To confirm my recollection, I asked my parents if they ever considered what I wanted to do or be, versus what they wanted me to do or expected me to be. Their answer was "No, we never did." No wonder I have difficulty being spontaneous, expressing personal desires, and doing my own thing. I cannot remember one instance wherein they said, "Gee, I don't know, but let's find out" or "Maybe I'm wrong; what do you think?" The "you know we're always right and know what's best" messages prevailed.

At one point in my teens, I suggested it made sense for me to go into the army, rather than back to college, since I wasn't sure of the career course I wanted to take. They responded, "No way! Nobody who goes into the army ever goes back to college." At the time, I didn't know how wrong they were. They needed to be right in order to hide their own shame issues about being inadequate and incapable. They had no idea they were passing the same issues on to me.

POWER

Most victims will switch to being victimizers, given the opportunity. What better way to act out a suppressed desire for power than to be an all-powerful god over a captive child? Finally my parents had a sense of power. "You'll do what I tell you to, or else" is encoded forever in my memory bank. The exertion of blatant power prohibited me from feeling that I had any rights, and prevented me from developing any healthy sense of power. Power in my family symbolized my position as a subordinate slave. It induced resentment and rebellion, and encouraged isolation and aloneness. My parents' inappropriate use of power signals how threatened they were by my existence and evolvement.

RAGE

This "I don't know how else to handle it, or what else to do, but I need to get my way" parenting technique exhibits "out of control anger," used threateningly to get someone's attention and to elicit a predictable response. It truly put the fear of God in me when either of my gods became irrationally angry, especially when I was involved. It was very damaging, destroying my sense of safety and security, inducing unreasonable fears instead. I now see that rage was the behavior of a little kid called daddy or mommy or sister, who said "I want my way at all cost, and will use my power to get it, regardless of the consequences." Today, I still have an unreasonable fear of someone "losing it" in my presence.

"Control by suppression" sums up my parents' basic technique. Their suppressive messages and the behavior that accompanied them formed the core of the degraded self-perception that became my shame-based false self. Sadly, I long perceived it as the real me. The type of behavior I experienced I now call "toxic." It was and is poisonous to my best interests and highest good. Toxic people take irrational thoughts and make them seem logical and rational. They're acting out of their survival instincts and issues, concerned only with their own agenda. When they profess love and care, it's generally used to disguise or cover up their controlling behavior. When parents use the above conditions to break the spirit of a child, they are committing soul murder.

THE RESULTS

My family environment induced a variety of character traits in me. In exploring them, I've deduced that certain ones are the result of my growing up in an environment where the parents were basically emotionally immature and insecure. They modeled magical beliefs about life and immature coping skills, instead of growth and responsibility.

Other character traits were imparted because my family was fear- and shame-bound, advocating criticism, judgment, self-righteousness, and blaming in an environment of perfection. We were pitted against each other, competing instead of complementing one another. The family focus centered on power, control, and the need to be right, negating the potential for harmony and peace. As a victim of this environment, I became fear- and shame-bound, set up to recycle self-defeating thoughts, feelings, and behaviors. I acquired the following characteristics, and explain what I believe caused them:

- Naïveté

    Sheltered from reality, with simplistic explanations about life's issues

- Unrealistic (magical) belief systems

    Immature parents, not in touch with reality

    Survival necessity due to criticism and shaming instead of support and caring

- Immaturity

    Lack of mature role models exhibiting mature coping skills

    Emotional abandonment

    Environment supporting pain avoidance and irresponsibility

- Irresponsibility

    Immature, passive parents permitting irresponsible family behavior, such as blaming

    Having had wants met instead of needs

- Insecurity

    My fear-based parents did not model a safe and secure atmosphere

    Their inflicting self-doubt versus self-confidence

    Feeling all alone, with no one truly on my team

- Pain avoidance/escape from reality

    Family dynamics that support rationalizations about reality and pain-avoidance techniques

    Attempts to relieve my guilt, fear- and shame-ridden false self of its painful feeling reality

- Compliance

    Doing whatever, to get the love I desperately needed in a family that professed conditional love

    Fostered by the threat of abandonment or pain when not meeting parental demands or desires

    Needing to be a "good little boy" to get my needs met

- Unreasonable fears

    Insecure parents, concealing and rationalizing their fears, passing them on

    Sensing that no one is on my team

    Excessive self-doubt

    My lack of sense of power, due to need to be compliant

- Competitive

  Attempting to prove worthiness

  Belief in scarcity

- Unreasonable self-centeredness

  An environment with unreasonable insecurity, fear, and shame

  Survival-based competing environment

- Hypervigilance

  The product of needing to "walk on eggshells" regarding others' feelings and behaviors

- Rebellion/defiance

  Realizing my parents weren't on my team and didn't consider my best interests and highest good as an autonomous human being

- Loneliness

  Lack of healthy bonding and no healthy mirroring
  A competing environment

- Unreasonable need to prove or protect

  Continued attempts to show that I am worthy and capable, while guarding my shame-bound false self

- Arrogance

  My mind's (ego's) attempt to offset my shame-ridden false self

- Free-floating disconnectedness

  Being disassociated from parts of myself that I separated from in my need to develop a false self and avoid pain

  Lack of healthy bonding and therefore a sense of not belonging

- Defensiveness

  A survival response to continuous boundary violations in a competing atmosphere

  Response to betrayal and deceitful behaviors

- Boredom

  No means for inspiration from my compliant false self due to lack of self-confidence, self-expression and ability to risk

- Distrust

  In an arena where all family members feel pitted against each other, no medium for trust exists

  Betrayal and deceit behaviors justified by family members

- Shut down feelings (fear of intimacy)

  No respect for boundaries

  Loss of trust

  Discord and pain disguised as functional

  Shaming by family members

- Secrecy

  Fear of exposure of shame

If you relate to having similar characteristics, please know that they are the result of your family environment, not some inherent defect in your being. I hope you will be able to see that the characteristics you have are the product of what you perceived you needed to do or your responses to how you felt, based on the circumstances of your family environment. We needed to survive, while getting our needs met in some way. Our need to survive also dictated that we conceal our fear and shame-based false selves from others and ourselves. We believed that that's who we really were.

I've surmised that my parents' inability to convey love lies at the root of all my problems. Hearing the words of love, without the deeds that support its presence, I acquired a distorted perception about what love is and what it means. This has caused much confusion and many difficulties for me. I felt, if I am loved, yet feel the way I do and deserve this, I must really be defective and bad at the core of my being. This was soul murder, plain and simple.

As children, we needed a sense of recognition, a sense of importance, a chance to earn respect and to be accepted. In some way, we achieved this in our families. However, the self-compromise and games required to accomplish the task promoted the formation of attributes similar to those I've previously mentioned. These attributes may have worked, been necessary, or gained approval in my family of origin, but most of them do not enhance functional and harmonious interactions with my fellow man. I call them my "dysfunctional survival [or coping] skills," necessary to survive and function in my family, but in general, not functional or healthy.

ADMIT TO OVERCOME

I've engaged the process of "name it, claim it, and tame it," where I've chosen to expose these traits rather than hide, protect, and justify them. I finally realized that these traits are the attributes that provide for a self-defeating lifestyle. In my quest for peace, love, and healthy, harmonious relations with my fellow man, I've needed to change many of these survival-oriented behaviors. I was not very willing to do this until I realized that they were a product of my family environment, not some inherent defect in me. Until then, I was fervently engaged in denial and justification games, guarding myself from the shame attacks that said these characteristics were inherent defects of my being. In attempting to change my behavior, I also needed to change the type of people I surrounded myself with, opting only to interact with those who would honor who I am and support my new effort.

In attempting to elude the thought that there really was something wrong with me, I have used many means to avoid the pain, shame, and fear messages that continued to gnaw at me. I didn't understand that by avoiding these feelings deep in my gut, I was disassociating from parts of me, contributing to my feelings of being disconnected. When I realized that these painful feelings were those I needed to escape from in my childhood, in order to survive, I was finally willing to embrace and process them. As I do, I inherently reclaim the parts of me that I detached from so long ago.

The dynamics in our families, such as they were or are, prohibited many of us from establishing healthy self-respect, self-esteem, self-worth, and healthy and functional coping skills. Only when children do not have to compromise themselves and their developmental process in order to get their needs met can they acquire functional coping skills and achieve healthy self-respect, self-esteem, and self-worth, the cornerstones of self-actualization.

Anytime parents use their children as tools to satisfy unfilled or current needs, they severely damage the child. If a parent uses the child to satisfy his or her insecurity or a need for worth, the child is being forced into an inappropriate role, that becomes its false self. When this happens, the child is being used, not honored and cared for, and its healthy development of a real self is severely interrupted.

It's unfortunate that many well-intentioned parents aren't emotionally equipped to handle the experience and the responsibility they've accepted. However, these immature and irresponsible parents need to be identified as such, rather than allowed to justify their behavior at the expense of innocent children.

7

ON BEING RESPONSIBLE

"What I haven't dealt with, I will pass on."

I've talked at length about my childhood and the parental dynamics involved in my family of origin. However, I too was a parent, responsible for raising two delightful children who became trapped in my generational malaise. In reviewing my ex-wife's and my parenting efforts, I'm saddened by the issues and ignorance on our part, and can clearly see the impact our efforts had in both my son's and daughter's lives. I could say that we didn't know any better, but that doesn't relieve the pain I feel when I reflect on what happened or what I've seen when watching home movies. In one instance during a picnic, my three-year-old son came running up to me crying, grabbing my leg. I continued my discussion with another man, only acknowledging my son's dilemma, not responding to it. As I viewed the clip, with pain in my gut, I said to myself, "Why didn't I pick him up and console him?" I hurt even more when concluding that my need to impress the person I was talking to overshadowed my desire to satisfy my son's needs.

My wife seemed to claim our daughter for her own from the very beginning. It promoted enmeshment between them, leaving my son and me somewhat out of their experience. I feel I have never really gotten to know my daughter, that I have never truly been part of her life, even though I was physically there and have tried to be close to her.

Although I was somewhat available for my children, I was generally preoccupied with my own agenda in much the same way my parents had been. Not having a contented real self, I was obsessed with my need to establish and maintain a satisfactory image for the world to see. And since my marriage had not been born out of love, I didn't encourage a happy family atmosphere. Outside of the family, I was gregarious and put together. At home, I was aloof and unavailable, except for certain instances when I'd tune in to the heartbeat of a situation with care and concern. In general, my message was "I don't have time right now,"— signaling emotional unavailability.

My preoccupation with covering up and counteracting my fear and shame-based false self took its toll on my children. Then, when they were nine and ten, I insisted on divorce, threatening them both with abandonment. They were also emotionally abandoned by their mother at the same time, as she struggled to deal with our divorce. Then came the blame and shame games, where the kids were used as pawns. During this time, they also witnessed my dependence on alcohol and the effect it had on me. Their sense of safety and security had been severely threatened, their beingness indelibly altered by our behavior and messages, as well as the pain of their experience.

A CHANCE TO MAKE AMENDS

Like my parents, my wife and I were not mature or functional enough to carry an untarnished message of love to our offspring. Our shortcomings, compounded by the discord of our relationship, conveyed distorted messages and beliefs to our children, which must inevitably create difficulties in their lives. I can honestly say that my wife's and my intentions were honorable throughout. But does that save us from owning the consequences of our behavior, when the well-being of our children was involved? I think not. The pain I have felt and feel is mine to endure, not cover up and hide at my children's expense.

Since, as parents, we have caused it, I believe we are the key to correcting it. I have chosen to own the parental responsibility I bestowed on myself, admitting my mistakes and deficiencies and changing my behavior and attitudes. I have expressed my regrets and tried to act accordingly. I believe that as a perpetrator, I have a wonderful opportunity to amend the past and help my son and daughter shed the part of their shame-based false selves inflicted by me and my behavior.

Ironically, my efforts have also relieved some of the guilt I have felt. Even though it really hurt, I feel good about somehow gathering the courage to face the truth, instead of telling myself I did the best I could or denying that I did anything wrong. I acknowledge that I could have done better and have committed to do what's possible to heal the wounds my behavior caused. I can at least give my children the gift of truth, one my parents were unwilling or unable to give me. My continued willingness is prompted by knowing how much it would have meant to me if my parents had done the same.

I have felt much loss and pain over not having been able to reconcile my relationships with my mother, father, and sister. I finally reached the point where I could no longer sacrifice me or my truth in order to interact in my family. Following my last attempt at having my perspectives recognized and honored, I opted for peace instead of discord and quietly moved away from them. I could no longer condone their self-protective stance at my expense. They had continued to insist that we were a loving, caring, functional family, in spite of overwhelming evidence to the contrary. In essence, by refusing to honor and respect my truth, they were demanding that I stay in the false self role they had designed for me, one without rights or equal consideration. In standing up for my right to be heard and considered, unwilling to bend, I proclaimed my real self for the first time, to those who had caused my dilemma. I was no longer willing to sacrifice me, or my values, beliefs, and truths, for their sake.

Part of me has felt a great deal of compassion for the role my parents played. Other parts of me feel pain, anger and loss. But since my parents continually refused to honor or respect my views, the adult in me has felt relief, not loss over our separation, because my inner children were no longer vulnerable to their beliefs and behaviors. I sensed that they cheered the fact that someone had finally stood up for what had really happened to them.

I'm convinced that if parents can "come clean" with their children, and honor and understand their children's perspective, relationships can be amended and healed, for the children and for the generations to come. It's never too late. If my parents could have garnered the courage to own their humanness and their deficiencies at any time in their lives, I believe their doing so would have had a healing effect on my wounds, which could not have been achieved in any other way.

As children, I'm suggesting that we finally demand the consideration we were due from the very beginning. And, as parents, I'm simply asking us to own the responsibility we bestowed on ourselves.

In owning my behavior and communicating it to my son, I have committed with him to making every effort to stop the generational dysfunction that infects our family tree. We have pledged to confront the problems and ourselves, instead of justifying twisted games, rationalizing their effect. We have promised to shoot straight with each other and own our own stuff, being accountable for our part. He is a father with two children, who like we, were perfectly wonderful seeds at birth. And, he still has the opportunity to make a difference at the beginning of their valuable lives.

EVALUATING RELATIONSHIPS

We've pondered and discussed the differences between functional and healthy, and dysfunctional and unhealthy. In creating a paradigm of healthy versus unhealthy attributes, we established a vision of parenting that could take us past trial and error, and beyond the dysfunctional norms of our society. With this vision, we would have the opportunity to turn our intentions into results. For those interested in the differences, I offer the following:

Functional (healthy)	Dysfunctional (unhealthy)
Accountable	Blaming
Humility	Self-righteousness
Validating	Critical
Humanistic	Perfectionistic
Complementary	Competitive
Freedom	Possession
Equality	Domination
Human value	Objectification
Security-based	Fear-based
Rules that support human rights	Rules that suppress human rights
Honor and innocence	Shame (judgment)
Interdependency	Codependency and enmeshment

Using the preceding yardsticks, I can look at the attributes of any family, business, association, church, school, or other group, and determine whether or not it promotes functional or dysfunctional lifestyles and beliefs. If I determine that I'm involved in a dysfunctional environment, I'd better understand that I'm a pawn in a game that doesn't have my best interests at heart and won't honor my highest good. In this instance, I'd better know that I'll have to struggle just to break even. As I evolve, I become less threatened by others or situations that I consider unhealthy or toxic. My eventual goal is having the capacity to convey the presence of love, regardless of what's going on around me or the situation I'm in.

HEALTHY STANDARDS

The above yardsticks will tell you about the environments you are or have been in. I hope they'll allow you to discern what's going on that might be about others instead of about you. But if you've come from a background similar to mine, where others would abuse me and my rights and make me feel that I deserved it, I understand the difficulty you might have in determining the difference.

Functional systems convey consideration, equality of rights, humanness, and responsibility. They honor the best interests of each person involved and their highest good. Some expressions communicated by these healthy attitudes:

> *"I don't know who's at fault here. Let's look at what happened, from both sides."*
>
> *"You have the same rights as anyone else, and that includes me."*
>
> *"I don't know the answer, but let's find out."*
>
> *"Maybe this isn't about you, or your fault."*
>
> *"That's neat. You do it uniquely."*
>
> *"It's not that you're bad, we just don't like this behavior."*
>
> *"When I said that, I was angry about . . . and I shouldn't have taken it out on you."*
>
> *"I screwed up, and I'm sorry."*
>
> *"Hi, it's good to see you."*

The preceding expressions indicate mutual consideration, equality of rights, humanness, and healthy responsibility. They are the attributes of functional behavior. The comments represent an attitude of rational maturity and love, untainted by perfectionism, criticism, blame, righteousness, and communicative games. I hope you can reflect on how hearing the above messages might present a different picture to you or someone else.

When I realized that most of us are lacking a sense of worthiness, importance, and recognition, I became determined to be one little ray of hope dedicated to changing the dysfunctional norm that permeates our society. I've learned that when I'm capable of displaying the humility and consideration necessary to validate and support others, miracles will follow. There's no secret here. It's just the way love works—we get what we give, and responsibility equals freedom.

8

≈

FAMILIES OF CHOICE

"If only love is real, then why not real love?"

WHY A FAMILY OF CHOICE?

Having attended over three thousand self-help meetings, I sensed that there was still an important ingredient missing for me. I had finally realized that I was a shame-based codependent who had reached an addictive phase of codependency called alcoholism (addiction). I came to realize that being shame-based fathered my codependency. I was like a furnace with a pilot light that had never worked, so I couldn't come to life by myself. Since my pilot light didn't work, my thermostat couldn't either; therefore I became dependent on others or things to turn me on or off and regulate my temperature. And, since my pilot light had never worked, I didn't realize that it should.

Having been raised in a shame-bound family with no cohesive support, I had never learned to believe in or trust myself. I had always felt that it was them against me or every man for himself. I was trapped in a continuous cycle of needing either to prove, impress, or protect, with no sense of what it would be like to just "be."

I had learned that whether I like it or not, left alone in my own mental and emotional environment, the messages of my past will eventually begin to erode any good feelings I've acquired about myself or my life. Self-confidence will eventually be supplanted by self-doubt. I finally understood that the self-talk that asserted that I was unworthy and incompetent always seemed to win, because it came out of my family of origin and was the essence of my false self. The struggles in my life were a series of self-defeating situations and circumstances generated by my self-defeating thoughts, feelings, and behaviors. And these self-defeating conditions were the result of the fear- and shame-bound truths that were deeply imbedded in my false self.

I needed what I'd never had—a family with a truly functional premise, with members who could commit to the actions of mature unconditional love. Also, since my codependency meant that I needed others to tell me who I was, it made sense to use my codependent traits in an effort to heal myself. If I could set up an environment wherein others would affirm, support, and believe in me, then maybe I could start doing the same, lighting my own pilot light for the first time.

I developed the "family of choice" premise, structure, and format in an attempt to provide the following:

- An atmosphere in which to build trust with others and myself.

- A sense of a functional family, with cohesive support.

- Consistent messages affirming that I'm okay and enough, just as I am.

- A safe setting for others and myself to share our innermost reality, risking intimacy.

- A base of unconditional love and support, necessary to foster healthy growth and maturity.

- A condition wherein the maintenance of an individual's rights and recovery are more important than the maintenance of the group.

It is my hope that the principles outlined here will give

you healthy guidelines for your relationships of any kind, even if you do not set up your own family. You can set up a family of choice with as few as two members. Most important to me is that I have a few relationships with people who have committed, in kind, to healthy, functional, and mature principles. Whether in a group setting or in everyday communication, they are the brothers and sisters of my family of choice. They are now my family, and they enhance my healing and evolution toward being what I believe I was intended to be. I suggest that those involved be other than a girlfriend, boyfriend, or significant other.

THE PREMISE

Many of us have struggled at living, not knowing why. We have not been able to make our lives work for us in a way we feel good about. We seem to continually get involved with or establish unhealthy, self-defeating situations and relationships. We simply don't seem to be able to promote ourselves toward our own best interests and highest good. Although many of us get along well with others, individually we often have a discouraging relationship with ourselves and our Creator, should we believe there is one. Our self-concept is generally not good or it is nonexistent. We labor at being okay or enough, and we find it most difficult to attain self-respect, self-esteem, and self-enjoyment.

A base of mature love is the foundation from which growth occurs. Since we didn't know it was absent from our past, our growth has been thwarted, leaving us insecure and immature, with limited coping skills. This void, combined with the shaming conditions that did exist, left us with little hope and few tools with which to build a successful life.

But in our family of choice we will see that how we feel about ourselves and how we think others feel about us are the results of the treatment we received and the programming inflicted on us in our childhoods. We will realize that today's fears and shame are illusions carried with us from the past in the form of our false selves. We will come to understand that who we were told we were is not us, but rather a false self inflicted on us, which we've believed as real. We will come to know in truth that we are, and always have been, innocent, worthy, talented offsprings of our Creator.

Because of our history, we have distorted perceptions about love and trust and their workings in a family or social environment. It is our hope here to establish a condition we've not experienced, a functional family based on unconditional love.

We all have abused children living within us. We hope to connect with them, identify what happened, and reparent them. To reparent ourselves in a healthy way, we will need the capacity of a loving mature adult capable of the task. Otherwise, we will have kids raising kids again and simply be enacting an illusion of recovery.

We believe that the conditions we have set forth for the group are functional acts of love that nurture and foster healthy principles. Mature self-discipline and a commitment to the principles are the cornerstones.

Our walk into spiritual maturity and healthy identities involves:

- A functional concept of "fair."
- Not taking sides.
- Being able to take an emotional gut hit without reacting or being immobilized.
- Respecting the other person's position when stating one's own.
- Honoring the differences.
- Acting in an honorable, accountable, and responsible manner.
- Valuing the "highest good" of all involved as a primary concern.
- Delaying gratification.
- A commitment to truth at all cost.

- Understanding that there is no good or bad, or right or wrong.

- Actions based on "knowing" versus "I wanna" or "I don't wanna."

FORMATION AND FORMAT

SUGGESTED GROUP SIZE: Two to eight people—male and female, all male, or all female; but not including an intimate mate.

TIME: Any time that's convenient for all. We meet each Monday at 7:30 P.M. and we just happen to be done by about 9:30 P.M. Each group will have its own personality and therefore its own time table.

HOW TO PICK MEMBERS: This can be a tough one. Know that you are choosing your brothers and/or sisters, people with whom you'd like to establish trust. I'd suggest that you only ask someone you feel connected to—someone with whom you feel you have a lot in common—someone you feel has the same sort of problems with life that you do.

GROUP FORMAT: We generally arrive at my apartment clubhouse, fifteen to thirty minutes early, for a cup of coffee and some general comraderie.

At 7:30 we sit down together and pass out the preface and group purpose statement. Someone will just start by identifying himself or herself, then read the beginning paragraph of the "Family Purpose Statement." When that's done, the person on the left or right will do the same, reading the next paragraph, with the process going on until the statement is finished. It then gets quiet. Someone will start by identifying himself or herself, then talk about some issue or condition that is on his or her mind. We normally share for from two to five minutes. When that person is finished, we thank him or her, and it gets quiet again, until someone else decides to share. We normally give everyone a chance to share once before anyone will share a second time. We continue until no one has anything else to share. We generally wind up in a small discussion about a prevalent issue that got brought up in the sharing. When finished, we form a circle of hugs and say a prayer together or just share our connectedness.

Members, as part of sharing, can ask the group to discuss a particular topic or issue that interests, concerns, or confuses them. The response to this request normally takes place toward the end of the meeting. A member, as part of sharing, can also ask for feedback from the group. This normally takes place at the time requested and only invites experiential responses, not evaluative ones.

Each group will have its own personality, the only common denominator being that they are all nonthreatening and focus on validation, support, and acceptance of one another.

PURPOSE STATEMENT
(Read at each meeting)

We have gathered primarily to work through and limit the negative impact of "shame" and "fear" in our lives. We will expose them, as manifested in our individual environments, exploring their origin and confronting them as illusionary lies perpetrated in our past. We will see that our shame-bound false selves were inflicted with lies about who we are. We will opt instead to nurture the precious real us that has lived on in secret. We will also explore our ego defenses, which have served us well in survival, but don't lend themselves to functional harmony and connectedness.

We insist that our family be "safe," that we maintain an atmosphere in which trust can be established and maintained. Since our paramount fears are of being judged and criticized, we should hope they be absent from our meeting. We also insist that we not give advice and that we phrase our comments so that they pertain only to ourselves.

Because "shame" manifests feelings of inadequacy, unimportance, and unworthiness, we shall each make a commitment to modify these negative illusions by honoring the preciousness, perfection, worthiness, and God-likeness in each other.

We will attempt to help each other see that the negative feelings we have about ourselves are simply negative illusions that bear no truth.

We ask that you leave your "self-criticism" outside, and not bring it into the meeting. Doing so will give you a better opportunity to see the valuable person that you are.

We have spent much of our time and effort looking for recognition, a sense of importance, and approval in an attempt to prove to others and ourselves that we are important and of value. In doing so, we've been most vulnerable to people and situations outside of us. Our purpose here, both individually and as a family, is to validate and support each other's importance and value just as we are, when we're not "doing" anything. We also support the premise that a higher power or supreme intelligence is guiding each of us toward our highest good, that each one of us knows what's right for himself or herself, requiring only validation, support, and acceptance of who we are to bring it into our lives. By honoring this belief with each other, it is our hope that we will ingest a new and positive truth about ourselves, replacing the negative thoughts that fear and shame have murmured throughout our lives.

We ask each other to honor our boundaries and our truth, in that we are precious, worthwhile descendants of our Creator, no matter what we say, know, or do. We also ask that there be no criticism or judgment, and that we refrain from giving advice unless asked, and then only share our personal experience.

TOPICS FOR DISCUSSION

How you relate to _____, and what it
means to you.

Abandonment	God or a supreme being
Betrayal	Self-centeredness
Commitment	Respect
Shame	Success
Sin	Anger
Loyalty	Failure
Fear	Defensiveness
Power	Codependency
Righteousness	Rage
Blame	

Pick any other issues or topics I've explored in the book,
and express your views about them, what they mean to you,
and how they might reflect on your childhood or your
thoughts or beliefs today.

THE TWELVE STEPS FOR A
RECOVERING HUMAN BEING

1. Admitted that I am powerless over my self-defeating thoughts, feelings, and behavior, and that my life has become unmanageable.

   (or)

   Admitted that I am powerless over my need for _____, and my life has become unmanageable.

   (or)

   Admitted that I am powerless over my need to _____, and my life has become unmanageable.

   (or)

   Admitted that I am powerless over my fear of _____, and my life has become unmanageable.

2. Came to believe that a power greater than myself could or could help me solve my dilemma.

3. Made a decision to trust in the care and guidance of a higher power or supreme intelligence, as I choose to perceive it.

4. Took an honest inventory of myself and my history.

5. Admitted to myself, my higher power, and a trusted other person what I had uncovered and discovered about myself and my life.

6. Became entirely ready to have my higher power do for me what I could not do for myself.

7. Sincerely asked my higher power to guide and help me.

8. Made a list of all persons whom I felt had violated or harmed me and whom I felt I had violated or harmed, and became willing to set it right with them all.
      (or)
   Made a list of all situations wherein I had violated my value system, and became willing to amend my part, in all cases.

9. Took the necessary actions to honorably correct or complete all of these situations, both past and present, except when to do so would not honor the highest good of others or myself.

10. Continued to take personal inventory, promptly addressing any discord, dysfunction, or self-defeating nuances.

11. Continued to improve my conscious contact with my higher power or supreme intelligence, as I perceive it, asking for the knowledge of its will for me and the power to carry that out.

12. Having had a spiritual awakening as the result of these steps, we began to enjoy our lives while practicing these principles in all our affairs.

THE TWELVE STEPS
OF ALCOHOLICS ANONYMOUS

1. We admitted we were powerless over alcohol—that our lives had become unmanageable.

2. Came to believe that a Power greater than ourselves could restore us to sanity.

3. Made a decision to turn our will and our lives over to the care of God as we understood him.

4. Made a searching and fearless moral inventory of ourselves.

5. Admitted to God, to ourselves and to another human being the exact nature of our wrongs.

6. Were entirely ready to have God remove all these defects of character.

7. Humbly asked him to remove our shortcomings.

8. Made a list of all persons we had harmed, and became willing to make amends to them all.

9. Made direct amends to such people wherever possible, except when to do so would injure them or others.

10. Continued to take personal inventory and when we were wrong promptly admitted it.

11. Sought through prayer and meditation to improve our conscious contact with God, as we understood him, praying only for the knowledge of his will for us and the power to carry that out.

12. Having had a spiritual awakening as the result of these steps, we tried to carry this message to alcoholics, and to practice these principles in all our affairs.

AFTERWORD

I fully recognize that many of my views in this book will seem radical to many in our society. If so, it only tells me where we're not and which denial games we still play. My writings are not about blame or parent-bashing, as some might suggest. They're about reality and healing. If they seem at another's expense, it is unintentional. These words may seem shocking because what happened is shocking.

I hope my book serves as a wake-up call to the issues of cause and effect, noting that they're in play regardless of our intentions or what we might choose to rationalize and justify. Our tendency is to treat the symptoms, not the cause, and to blame others. Like the national debt, we can talk about it all we want, suppose what we wish, and blame whom we might. But the erosion keeps gnawing away at us, as evidenced by the pervasive increase in crime and addiction.

As a society, we seem surprised and disheartened when children become prostitutes, addicts, gang members, robbers, street persons, murderers, wife beaters, manic-depressives, schizophrenics, or psychotics. Parents everywhere cry "After all we did for him [or her]," seemingly ignorant of any clue about what they've given cause to. I believe we could examine the family environment and the players involved, and in each case determine the particular outcome as predictable and most obvious. It's time we understood that well-meaning is not well-producing, that treating symptoms does not treat problems, and that blame doesn't solve anything.

As a responsible farmer, I can't be fooled anymore by anyone proclaiming there are bad seeds. Since I've come to know there are none, I can't be conned into thinking that the watering provided, the pruning, and the particular fertilizer used weren't the causes for a poor crop. I'm on to the little blame games and I can see under the mask of self-righteous rationalization and deceit. I now understand the laws of cause and effect, and more important, I know where the seeds come from in the first place. And believe me, there are none made short of perfect.

I hope my sharing has afforded you some new perspectives that will enhance your life. I hope I've converted some self-doubt into self-confidence, some degrading shame-based perceptions into a sense of innocence, personal defects into necessary survival instincts, a lack of faith and trust into abandonment or betrayal issues, and your perceived flawed self into an inflicted false self that is not you. Deep down inside each of us, underneath the rubble of fear, shame, pain, and grief, there is a spark that nobody could have ever touched or tarnished. And regardless of how we feel or where we are today, this spark is still alive and well in each of us. It is the real us, perfect and pure and innocent. As we nurture it, care for it, defend it, and encourage it to grow, this perfect expression will germinate and begin to blossom. As it does, the faint whisper of "I am" will grow louder and louder.

COMPLEMENTARY READING MATERIAL

Beattie, Melody. *Codependent No More: How to Stop Controlling Others and Start Caring for Yourself.* Walker and Company, 1989.

Bradshaw, John. *Healing the Shame That Binds You.* Health Communications, Inc., 1988.

Forward, Susan. *Toxic Parents: Overcoming Their Hurtful Legacy and Reclaiming Your Life.* Bantam, 1990.

Hay, Louis L. *You Can Heal Your Life.* Hay House, 1987.

Miller, Alice. *Banished Knowledge: Facing Childhood Injury.* Doubleday, 1991.

Patent, Arnold. *You Can Have It All.* Celebration Pub., 1991.

Peck, M. Scott. *The Road Less Traveled: A New Psychology of Love, Traditional Values, and Spiritual Growth.* Simon and Schuster, 1980.